Best Practices of Effective Nonprofit Organizations

A PRACTITIONER'S GUIDE

Philip Bernstein

The Foundation Center

LIBRARY OF CONGRESS CATALOGING-IN-PUBLICATION DATA

Bernstein, Philip, 1911–
    Best practices of effective nonprofit organizations : a
practitioner's guide / Philip Bernstein.
        p.   cm.
    Includes index.
    ISBN 0-87954-755-3
    1. Nonprofit organizations—Management.   I. Title.
    HD62.6.B48   1997
    658′ .048–DC21

                                                    97-618
                                                    CIP

Contents

FOREWORD

For more than a decade, I had urged Phil Bernstein to put in writing his extraordinary experience in leading voluntary organizations. This was not just a reflection of admiration of his accomplishments but also an awareness of the urgent need to have a written record of the experience and advice of some of the great nonprofit practitioners. As the field grows in importance and size, we have to capture and apply the lessons of those who demonstrated remarkable ability to build organizations and that were a match for the great needs and aspirations of their times. Phil Bernstein was the best of the best, and I was determined to get him to provide a written account.

Initially, Phil wrote about his unique view and experience relating to the Jewish federation movement in the United States which culminated in his first-rate volume, *To Dwell in Unity*. When he asked me to critique an early draft of it, I expressed delight he was doing it, commendation on the progress, but concern that it was too clinical and scholarly, obscuring his warm and practical voice. We later talked at length about my view of his rare combination of practitioner and communicator and the need for those attractive and persuasive attributes to come to the fore in his writing. He needed to be persuaded, not out of stubbornness, but because of self-effacing doubt that he was really unique and an optimistic expectation that the facts should speak for themselves. But he listened and revised and the result was a much better book because it was much more Bernstein.

Several years later—about three years ago—Phil called to say he had finally drafted a more general book that we had talked about to address the broader spectrum of voluntary organizations. He wanted to know if I would read it and be equally candid with reactions. In subsequent correspondence and conversations, I was not equally frank. I was even more critical. I acknowledged and praised the fact that all of the basics were present, except the real Phil Bernstein. Once again, his modesty and faith smothered the reality that what would make every message and lesson in his book truly galvanizing was *his* personal experience, *his* heartbreaks, *his* thrills, and *his* ability to put it all on the line with candor and conviction.

Frankly, I didn't expect him to revise his material to anything like the degree proposed. The book was too far along; he was too senior in status to have to listen to criticism; and I was asking him to come out front where he was never really comfortable. I was absolutely wrong. I was not dealing with anything like the average person. I was dealing with Bernstein. Even at his age and seniority, he went back to what any author would recognize as an excruciatingly unpleasant task: to tear apart one's masterpiece and redo it to someone else's standards.

The fact that he did it says a great deal about his humanity, openness, and conscientiousness, and the fact that he did it so well says even more about his lifelong ability to persevere to reach the very best result for the task at hand.

The book turned out to be his final major task. Phil died just after the manuscript was submitted to the Foundation Center. In what turned out to be our final conversation, when I called to tell him of my absolute delight with the final product, he couldn't quite accept that I would be so terribly satisfied, and especially that I had absolutely nothing further to suggest! I explained that I had been difficult only because he expected honesty, and now that I could hear and feel his heart and soul coming through, I had not a thing to add.

Phil described the book as "a practitioner's guide." It is the best of that, but it is much more. It is history, inspiration, and conscience. All of those characteristics come ringing through, especially his wisdom, gentleness, and absolute commitment to bring out the best that is within us to serve the public good. Phil was the nicest tenacious man I ever knew.

The book is real Phil Bernstein, prodding and teaching us to be better leaders of our causes and crusades. His legacy is now all the stronger because the book extends his reach and preserves his voice.

Brian O'Connell
April, 1996

1

A Practitioner's Guide

Nonprofit organizations differ greatly in their levels of achievement. The disparities are striking even among those that operate in the same fields, address the same or parallel needs, and share the same goals.

Some advance consistently, year after year, and they increasingly achieve more of their purposes. They obtain greater financial and volunteer support, and attract and retain outstanding professional staffs. They move ahead creatively and dynamically. In contrast, others progress more modestly or just inch forward; some stand still or even retreat.

Few organizations are satisfied with their status of achievements. The nonprofit sector is not complacent. Even the most productive organizations do not rest on their oars. They know that they are not meeting all the needs, that some of what they do should be done better, and that services that are excellent today may be outmoded in the near future because of advancing knowledge and skills. They constantly appraise their services and results, their strengths and weaknesses, the emerging challenges and opportunities. They press to do more, and to do it better.

They continually ask themselves: Are we making a real difference? In people's lives, in society? Are we making enough of a difference? Can we make a greater difference? How?

Underlying their discontent is their deep commitment to help raise the quality of life, to help build stronger and better societies. They cannot accept the erosion of family life, the neglect and lifelong damage that is inflicted on children, inadequate health care, growing pollution, discrimination against minorities, and barriers to cultural creativity.

The less-productive organizations ask: Why are we accomplishing less than the best groups? What do they do that we don't do? What do they do better? What mistakes do we make?

This ongoing search has been reinforced by pressures on nonprofit organizations that stem from the shrinking role of the federal government in providing human services and making financial grants to nonprofits. The pressures have been mounting for nonprofits to carry greater responsibilities, to operate most effectively, and to manage most efficiently.

Nonprofit organizations vary tremendously in the needs they address, in their services, in their scope and size, and in other ways. They range from small neighborhood associations to international enterprises; they are governed by boards that range from small self-perpetuating bodies of a half-dozen people to those with more than 200 members who are chosen by and accountable to mass constituencies.

Despite their disparities, the most advanced, productive nonprofits across the entire sector share principles, practices, and skills that are their hallmarks. The principles and practices are applied creatively and selectively to fit the circumstances of each organization. They are the bedrock of the eminent organizations. They provide the models from which others can learn and forge ahead.

These principles, practices, and skills and how they are applied, drawn from the experience of hundreds of nonprofits across America make up the substance of this book. These principles, practices, and skills are validated by the actions and judgments of preeminent leaders in the nonprofit field, both volunteer and professional. And they have been confirmed by my own experience over several decades as a professional staff member, executive, and consultant, and as a volunteer board and committee member in local, national, and international organizations.

This is a practitioner's manual, an exposition of some of the best of what is already being done and achieved. It is not a theoretical wish list. No organization applies all of these practices optimally, though many strive to.

It is a selected manual. I have not tried to compile an encyclopedia of all successful practices. Rather I have chosen those that often underlie the achievements of productive nonprofit organizations, and that exist in contrast to the mistakes and setbacks of other organizations, problems that could have been avoided if they had done what the leading organizations do.

Following are the selected elements that underlie, in large part, the successes of the leading nonprofit organizations.

They will be explained in the various chapters, as specified below.

Effective organizations have defined their purposes and goals, formalizing them in officially adopted mission statements. They know what they want to achieve. They adhere to their missions scrupulously, in order to concentrate on the services that are most important to achieve their goals. (Chapter 2)

The organizations place their greatest priority on obtaining and retaining the highest-quality volunteers and professional staffs. They have identified such people as the most important necessity for maximum effectiveness in everything they do. They have defined the respective roles of the volunteers and professionals, so that they can work together in a harmonious, productive partnership. (Chapters 3, 4, 5)

The organizations employ comprehensive financing, embracing several types of funding from various sources, to make their services possible. They have achieved a solid, stable underpinning of funds, often with consistent growth year after year. (Chapter 6)

The advanced nonprofits are alert to changes in needs and opportunities. They flexibly adjust their services and operations to these changes. (Chapter 7)

The organizations budget their funds to concentrate on the services that are most vital to the accomplishment of their goals. The budgets are based on thorough planning, which projects what can be done most productively in the year and years ahead, and which does not merely continue what has been done in the past. (Chapter 8)

Volunteers and staff are intensively involved in governance, management, decision making, implementation of decisions, and oversight and conducting of services. Boards and committees are active, essential, and productive instruments of involvement and progress. (Chapters 9 and 10)

Difficult, complex, and controversial major issues are often successfully resolved by clearly designed procedures that are skillfully employed. Decisions are usually made by consensus, unifying and strengthening the organizations, rather than permitting issues to fragment them. (Chapters 11, 12, 13)

Decisions are implemented fully. Implementation is monitored to make sure that actions faithfully carry out an organization's intent. Organizations evaluate their services and management to assess how effectively they are progressing toward their goals, and how fully they are accomplishing their purposes. (Chapters 14 and 15)

The best nonprofits carry out high-quality, planned, and carefully budgeted communication. This includes internal communication to volunteers, staff, and constituents, and external communication to the general public, the media, and government agencies. It is conducted as an essential ingredient of the organization's operations, and is designed to build understanding, involvement, commitment, and support. (Chapter 16)

Individual consultations with volunteers, staff members, and others are carried out intensively to obtain guidance, build mutual understanding and cooperation, prepare group deliberations, overcome differences, and resolve issues. (Chapter 17)

Leading organizations collaborate with other nonprofits on shared concerns and purposes, to achieve together what each could not accomplish alone. (Chapter 18)

The organizations actively guide government in enactment of legislation and regulations, and influence judicial decisions affecting nonprofit responsibilities, operations, financing, and services. (Chapter 19)

All of the above practices are related and interdependent. The effectiveness of each is made possible in part by the others, and is strengthened by them. (Chapter 20)

This manual provides a selection of guidelines that can be particularly helpful to the innumerable professional practitioners who are eager to advance their organizations to greater achievements. It is a selection that can have special value for teachers and for their students in academic and training programs as they prepare for lifelong professional service in nonprofit organizations, as well as for current practitioners in continuing professional education programs.

It is hoped that this manual will have widespread value for volunteer leaders regarding their own roles and their relationships with their professional staffs.

2

MISSION

Successful organizations know clearly what their mission is, what their goals are, and what they want to achieve. They adhere to their goals. They concentrate on them. They limit themselves to them.

They have formulated an official statement of their mission that has been thoroughly considered and adopted by their governing body. They continually refer to the mission statement, to test whether proposed new responsibilities conform to it.

The process of formulating and adopting the mission statement is important in itself. The process enables people to express their views and understanding of what should be the major purpose, goals, and responsibilities of the organization. It enables the organization to select those that have the greatest agreement and support. The participation, analysis, and discussion by volunteer leaders and staff deepens the organization's understanding and commitment to the mission.

Successful organizations are flexible in changing their priorities and activities within their mission. Indeed they are notable for initiating and creating such change. But when new responsibilities are proposed that are beyond their mission they reject them unless they deem them important enough to warrant a reappraisal of their mission. They examine whether other organizations already carry that responsibility or should more logically consider the proposed services. If not, they analyze what impact the revision of their mission would have on their current services, and whether they have the competence and resources to extend or alter their mission.

The more successful and prestigious an organization is, the greater and more frequent will be the pressures on it to undertake new responsibilities beyond its current scope and purpose. Such new responsibilities are often urged to address unmet needs. People dissatisfied with how other organizations are dealing with a problem will press a highly successful organization to take over and "do it right." Successful organizations frequently resist such pressure.

A mission statement is no guarantee in itself that an organization will adhere to its mission. Members of the organization may interpret the statement differently, stretching and rationalizing its meaning to include activities they want the organization to undertake. In this way, organizations can wander far from their basic purposes and from the competence of their volunteers and staff. I have seen organizations extend themselves into a succession of new responsibilities, functions, and services that are only remotely related to their central mission, if at all. The problem was that the staff, well qualified for what they were already doing, lacked the competence for the new areas.

They diverted funds from their priorities to conduct the additional activities, with the result that their activities overall became increasingly diffuse and superficial. They confused the understanding of their volunteer leaders about what they were trying to achieve. They reduced their effectiveness, washed out some of the respect they had earned, and weakened the loyalty and commitment of their leaders and supporters, who had been attracted by their previous concentration. They slid downhill, losing volunteers and funds.

In contrast, the leading organizations have learned that to be excellent in what they do does not automatically guarantee excellence in other realms. They have learned that bigness is not always best. They have not deviated from their commitment to achieve the utmost in what is most important to the organization.

Successful organizations schedule a periodic review of their mission statements to determine whether they continue to define their current central purposes or need revision. Such reviews are thorough analyses, in the depth of the reexamination and in the involvement of the leaders, board members, constituents, and staff. They review the circumstances that prevailed when the statement was adopted, and the underlying motivations, premises, and criteria on which it was based. They assess whether the organization's services have implemented the mission statement, the goals it was intended to achieve, and the actual results; the changing needs that challenge the organization; whether other organizations have adopted the same purposes and goals, and have been successful in acting upon them; the prevailing major concerns of constituents; and other elements.

Such a review is a deliberate process. It may begin with a board meeting at which members are asked to voice their views of the mission statement and bring forward their questions, comments, and suggestions, to help set the framework for the review.

A blue-ribbon committee composed of the foremost leaders and ablest newer members then takes account of these comments in examining whether the mission statement is relevant to the current purposes and goals of the organization. The committee may recommend reaffirmation of the statement, or modest or major revisions, or other options for consideration by the board. The board considers the committee's findings and recommendations, and works toward a consensus and adoption of a current mission statement. The board's action is a recommendation to the constituents for their consideration and action.

Many organizations have revised their mission statements so as not to remain frozen in an outmoded past:

EXAMPLE:
A major family-welfare organization ceased its counseling and other direct services and shifted to a concentration on research, public policy initiatives, and advocacy to improve human services more comprehensively.

EXAMPLE:
A number of foundations have made changes such as replacing many small grants with a few large ones, in order to make a greater impact; have revised the proportion of their funds allocated to domestic and overseas needs; and have selected three or four fields for

concentration, rather than spread their grants
over a broad spectrum.

A review process and action on the mission statement is
vital to an organization. The deepened understanding is
essential for both veteran and new board members, as well
as for constituents and staff. The mission statement is now
an expression of their mutually agreed purposes and goals,
not only something inherited from previous generations. It
is based on their knowledge and convictions, and has their
understanding and commitment. As a result, the organization is more focused, stronger, and more productive.

3

VOLUNTEER LEADERS

The most important determinant of the success of the leading nonprofits is their human resources—their volunteer leaders and professional staffs. Their quality and commitment, more than anything else, determines the strength and effectiveness of the organization. No nonprofit can be better than the people who comprise it and lead it. Their quality affects every element of the nonprofits.

The highest priority of nonprofits is the recruitment, training, involvement, and retention of the ablest volunteer leaders, and similarly of their professional staffs. Their recruitment and involvement is a thoroughly planned and skillfully executed process.

We'll look first at the volunteer leaders, and in the next chapter at the professional staffs.

Voluntary organizations are citizen organizations. Volunteers govern the nonprofits. They determine the policies, programs and services, and finances. They oversee the administration and operation. They are accountable for the organizations.

Successful nonprofit organizations have spelled out the qualifications necessary for people to become officers and members of their governing bodies. Some requirements are so basic that they are pervasive in the sector; others vary from organization to organization. The basic ones include the following considerations.

Commitment to the mission of the organization is primary. The organizations seek men and women who will invest the time and energy the responsibility requires—to do the reading and other homework, have the consultations, attend the meetings, and carry out the activities they are asked to undertake.

Such men and women insist on excellence in the organization's performance, and reject complacency and rigidity. They have vision and are flexible about the possibility of change, yet are realistic and practical when considering its feasibility. They are open to the differing views and aspirations of others, while vigorous in expressing their own judgments.

They are sensitive to the communities of which their organizations are a part. They exemplify the aspirations, values, and norms of their communities. They understand that they are accountable not only to their constituents, but to their communities.

They are highly regarded and respected by others. As Senator Daniel Patrick Moynihan has put it, "Some people meet standards; others set them." Effective volunteers influence others—the constituents of the organization, government officials, people within the power structure of the community. They are current leaders, not just past leaders.

They strengthen the organization with the expertise they bring from their businesses and professions, in law, accounting, management and administration, scholarship, and other vocations.

They understand the difference between the decision-making processes of voluntary organizations, business, and government. They are attuned to the sensitivities involved in overcoming differences and reaching consensus by persuasion, epitomized in the ancient Chinese poem that states "the best leadership is so graceful that people think it is they who have led."

A number of leading organizations have continuing structured and systematically implemented programs to identify and engage individuals with these qualities or potentials. They assign volunteer leaders and staff members who would have the most influence with each prospect to contact them, meet with them, deepen their understanding of the organization and its services, and effect their involvement in the planning, financing, services, and governance of the organization.

Their nominating committees, which officially select the candidates for election by the board or constituency to the governing bodies, are carefully chosen to represent a cross section of the organization. Committee members are informed of the criteria and qualifications, and adhere to them. They often function throughout the year to make a continuing canvass of the best potential prospects.

The procedures of the leading organizations contrast with those of less successful ones, which choose volunteers haphazardly and without criteria. Often board members merely propose their friends, who may or may not be qualified, and thus build ingrown, single-minded governing bodies that limit the range and experience of the organization, as well as its growth and achievement.

With their high standards, the leading nonprofits nevertheless are aware that many prospects do not come with all of the required attributes. Some may bring special strengths in particular knowledge and skills, in influence and relationships, in financial support. The best organizations conduct structured training programs to provide the required overall knowledge and skills. The new members are educated about the history of the organization; its mission, policies, and programs; its budget, board, committees, and staff structure and composition; and its operational procedures.

For both newly elected and veteran board members, board institutes and retreats are held to probe in depth major issues and emerging trends.

The leading organizations urge their board and committee members to participate in national, regional, and local conferences on the responsibilities of their organizations. They encourage their members to network with leaders of sister organizations and to inform them of their advances in knowledge and experience.

In order to assure a continuing inflow of new people with different ideas, views, and experience, successful organizations limit the number of consecutive years each board member can serve. They particularly strive to involve young people who want to help build the future society in which they especially have a particular stake. At the same time, such organizations assure the continued service of outstanding leaders after their formal board membership ends, through service on committees or on special projects, through consultations, and in other ways, so they do not lose the benefit of their invaluable abilities, experience, and influence. In some cases, they bring these leaders back on the board after a period off the board.

Leading organizations are deeply grateful for the services of their volunteers and convey their gratitude in many ways. The chief volunteer officers telephone and write people to express appreciation after they have performed a particularly noteworthy service. Volunteers are lauded publicly at board and annual meetings, and are given tangible tokens of gratitude. The tributes mean much to the recipients, encourage them to continue and increase their service, and set models for others to emulate.

How volunteers lead and serve most effectively is a theme that runs through much of the balance of this book.

4

———••◆••———

PROFESSIONAL STAFFS

Able volunteers are teamed with highly qualified staffs in the leading nonprofit organizations. Both are indispensable. Neither can function at their best without the other. They are interdependent.

The most highly qualified volunteers insist on having the strongest staffs. They do not tolerate mediocrity; they refuse to waste their time, and do not remain in organizations that plod along with poor staffs.

Pivotal is the chief professional officer (CPO). No person more vitally determines the effectiveness of a nonprofit than the CPO. I have seen nonprofits go downhill dramatically when an excellent CPO left and was replaced by a mediocre successor. By the same token, I have seen struggling organizations become outstanding achievers when average CPOs were replaced by splendid ones.

What distinguishes outstanding CPOs who work with the most productive organizations? They are expert in how nonprofit organizations function. They know how such organizations are structured and governed, the distinctive responsibilities of volunteers and professionals and how they work together, how the organizations are administered, and how their funds can be increasingly obtained and spent most effectively.

They know how the organizations can plan for the short term and the long term, how they can help shape their future and not just react to ad hoc pressures as they arise. They understand the requirements of accountability and carry them out.

They know how nonprofits resolve difficult issues and conflicts to reach consensus. They understand how to be initiators, enablers, and catalysts; they are skilled as harmonizers in finding the elements of agreement, and in helping to resolve the elements of disagreement. They carry out decisions effectively and productively.

They have a depth of knowledge and experience in the fields they serve, whether in the arts, child care, civil rights, health, environment, or others. They know the resources they can draw upon to augment their own knowledge and experience. They keep informed about the successful accomplishments of other organizations they can emulate or adapt, and about the failures of others they should not repeat.

They are deeply committed to their work. Their commitment makes a great difference in their attitudes and behavior. It affects how they confront difficulties—obstacles, complexities, conflicts, or setbacks. It determines whether they are frustrated, drained, or embittered by them, or can take them in stride with the resolve to overcome them.

Beyond their expertise in the field, they have become thoroughly knowledgeable about the organization that employs them—its mission, history, current status, policies, priorities, and services. They have learned what major issues have been debated, what the opposing positions were, who advocated them, and how they were resolved and why; if issues remained unresolved, they find out why.

Organizations that have employed CPOs on the premise that good managers can manage anything have learned to their sorrow that often they cannot. These organizations have glossed over the reality that managers who succeed know what they are managing, and that managers in nonprofit organizations are addressing what are often extremely difficult and complex problems.

This has been evident in instances where successful business executives have tried to become CPOs of nonprofit organizations, without getting special training for the nonprofit field. And it has been evident too when professionals in one field have become CPOs in other fields. For example, a very successful school superintendent who was employed as the CPO of a large welfare and health organization soon found and readily admitted that he was at a kindergarten level of knowledge in a position in which he was expected to direct and supervise a staff with postgraduate and professorial expertise. He could not lead or guide them when he did not know the basic elements of what they were doing. He had no experience in handling relationships with the volunteer leaders of a governing board of a nonprofit organization. He did not have a peer relationship with the CPOs of other organizations in the field with which his organization had to collaborate. In a few years, the organization and he agreed that it was a mutual mistake for him to have taken the position, and he left.

Together with professional expert knowledge and skills in their CPOs, the leading nonprofit organizations require personal qualities they believe are essential for the ablest, most effective executive service.

They want CPOs who are creative, who can look ahead to the potentials of higher goals and achievements; who can propose how to seek and accomplish them; who have vision and can inspire others with their creativity and initiatives.

They want people who are open—who can share concerns, test ideas, and ask for knowledge, judgment, and advice from others; who can listen, hear, understand, consider fairly, and respond.

They want CPOs who can administer and manage skillfully, who can get the greatest value from every dollar spent, who can match the highest management standards of the most efficient business, applying advanced technologies to their operations. They want CPOs who understand and utilize the new computer, communication, and other operational tools.

They insist on integrity and trust, on people whose word is their bond, who are completely honest in what they say and do, and who carry out their promises and commitments; people who win the confidence of opposing factions within an organization because of their fairness, objectivity, and empathy.

They require CPOs with high intelligence who can analyze issues and problems that are often entangled, who can command the respect of highly intellectual volunteers and other professionals. They have found that security and stability in their CPOs is essential; that the CPOs must confront and work through unforeseen obstacles and setbacks without losing their poise; that they must be able to handle calmly the criticism and even the attacks of people who oppose what the organization does and who may make the CPO the target of their attacks. They want CPOs who are well organized, who can handle multiple pressures smoothly and effectively.

And with personal relations so central to the responsibilities and success of CPOs, they want executives who are outgoing, at ease in meeting and relating to many types of personalities and people with different and opposing priorities, people who may be demanding, impatient, and even inflexible.

Along with these top-of-the-list qualities are others that mark the most highly regarded CPOs—qualities such as optimism; a refusal to believe that a problem is insoluble because of temporary roadblocks; and a sense of humor, especially when it can dissipate the tension of a difficult discussion.

No CPO should be expected to have all of these qualities, and any CPO will be stronger in some than in others. But the most successful executives know the importance of these requirements, and work to improve their strengths and overcome their shortcomings.

Because the quality of its leadership is so crucial to an organization, the selection of the CPO is the most critical decision the governing board will make. When the position is to be filled, the leading nonprofits employ a sophisticated search process. Its basic components are a search committee whose members are a cross section of the governing body and constituency, supported with professional assistance; a well-considered set of criteria by which candidates are judged, drawn up by the committee and governing body; an open process in which members of the governing body and constituency are encouraged to suggest individuals for consideration; the widest canvass to identify the most qualified people to be considered; and a thorough check of the previous work experience of candidates, not by written references alone, but by personal contacts to learn their weaknesses and strengths.

The committee conducts interviews with the leading candidates as a two-way process, in which the candidates may ask the committee as many questions about the organization and position as the committee asks about the candidates' qualifications. The committee or a subcommittee holds discussions with the person selected to work out the final terms of employment, as a recommendation to the governing body. After consideration of the committee's recommendation, the governing body makes an offer of employment. Between the time the decision is made and the date the new CPO assumes the responsibility, a systematic transition process takes place. Finally and very important, the organization warmly welcomes the CPO with gracious amenities and courtesies when he or she begins.

The strongest voluntary organizations not only have the ablest CPOs, but the best-qualified staffs as a whole. Outstanding CPOs attract, recruit, develop, and retain highly competent staffs. The staff members work under conditions and procedures that enable them to grow professionally and to serve with the highest morale. They are compensated appropriately for the outstanding vision, creativity, leadership, knowledge, and skills they provide the organizations. The compensation is at levels that will attract them, retain them, and express the continuing regard of the volunteer leaders for the advances the staff enables the organizations to make.

A personnel committee of the governing body provides oversight to policies, practices, needs, and changing requirements. The policies and conditions are formalized in a personnel code that the committee has developed with staff participation and that has been reviewed and adopted by the governing body. The code is used in ongoing supervision, in annual evaluations, and in filling vacancies. There are written job specifications for each position, so that the employer and the employee have a mutual understanding of the responsibilities.

The purpose of the continuing professional supervision is to help each staff member perform at his or her best, growing in capability and achieving at a consistently high level. Supervisory conferences are scheduled well ahead; supervisors keep their appointments meticulously, in contrast to the practice in weaker organizations where such appointments are frequently cancelled, conveying to the individual being supervised that other matters are more important, and undermining their commitment and morale.

The supervisors in the strongest nonprofits recognize that they need supervisory conferences for their own benefit, to keep informed of what the staff is doing, and with what success or difficulty or failure; to plan; to suggest changes in a timely fashion; to set future goals and target dates for future actions; to learn of new developments and consider what, if anything, should be done about them; and to provide leadership to the staff. A notable weakness of less successful organizations is the absence of such skilled, systematic supervision.

CPOs skillfully delegate responsibility, as well as the authority required by the responsibility, with trust and confidence. They respond promptly to staff reports, suggestions, and requests. CPOs continually keep the staff informed of new developments and seek their advice and judgment, not only on the respective responsibilities of each staff person, but on the work of the organization as a whole. Each staff member keeps the others informed of his or her work.

An abiding characteristic of the most successful organizations is the collegiality of the staff members. They work as a cohesive, cooperative, interdependent team. Staff members are involved in what will be brought to the governing body for consideration and action. If there is a strong division in their judgments, every effort is made to resolve the differences prior to consideration by the governing body. Irreconcilable differences, if important enough, may delay consideration or persuade the CPO not to bring the matter to the board, if that option is open.

Support staff members as well as those on the professional staff are kept informed of developments. They are made to feel essential to the progress and achievements of the organization.

The morale of the staff members is a paramount consideration. They are not anonymous cogs in an organizational wheel; they relate directly to volunteer leaders, report publicly on their significant work, and are identified and credited for their achievements. They have enthusiasm for what they do and what they try to accomplish, and the organization expresses regard and appreciation for their quality privately and publicly.

5

———•◦•—◦—•◦•———

VOLUNTEER AND
PROFESSIONAL
RELATIONS

A hallmark of leading nonprofit organizations is the intimate collaboration of their volunteer leaders and their
professional staffs. This collaboration is an integrated partnership based on their mutual support, on understanding
of what each contributes that the other cannot, of the responsibilities that are distinctive to each, and of the responsibilities that are shared and why. Each is indispensable to
the other. Each helps to enhance the capability of the other.

There is an understanding that the difference between
volunteers and professionals is not simply that volunteers

serve part-time and professional staffs full-time, or that volunteers serve without compensation and that professionals are paid. There is a recognition that there are basic differences in authority, responsibility, knowledge, experience, and skills.

Volunteers and professionals are completely agreed that the volunteers determine and are accountable for the policies, programs, and finances of the organization. They are responsible for having their decisions carried out. Their authority is clear: The professionals are bound by those policies and decisions.

But while the professionals do not make the decisions, they are vitally involved in the consideration and process of arriving at them. The volunteers depend upon them for the depth of their knowledge, experience, and expertise, and for their analyses. The volunteers ask the professionals to present options for resolving issues, and to delineate the merits and deficiencies of each. Subsequently, the volunteers invite and give special weight to the opinions of the professionals in arriving at their decisions.

Just as both volunteers and professionals are involved in the process of formulating policies and actions, both share in implementing them. The oft-repeated maxim that "volunteers make decisions, professionals carry them out" is only partly true. Successful implementation often requires the leadership and involvement of volunteers. They have personal, business, and political relationships and influence, especially with people in power, that are crucial. They have knowledge and skills that professionals do not possess.

In order for them to apply these assets with full commitment and determination, volunteers must be fully involved in, and responsible for, the determination of the policies and decisions. Their full understanding and support must underlie the decisions. The volunteers are not rubber stamps for the professionals. They have not been manipulated by the professionals, nor could they be.

> EXAMPLE:
> An organization was operated entirely by
> volunteers in its first years. They performed
> with such commitment, ability, and success
> that the responsibilities grew to the point that
> they could not give the greater time required.
> They agreed that a full-time professional
> should be employed, especially to carry out the
> further expansions they had projected.

They engaged a person with an outstanding record in business and government. He splendidly carried out the current programs and the further growth the volunteers had planned.

He then presented to a meeting of the board a blueprint of additional programs he had creatively designed, in full detail. Substantially greater income would be required, which he also specified precisely, including the contribution each board member would make, as well as the fund-raising quota each would carry.

At this point the board firmly balked. They told him that they had not been consulted in the formulation of his plans, had no prior knowledge of them, had no responsibility for them, no basis for making the contributions requested, and no commitment on which to base a solicitation of others. The plan was "dead on arrival."

The best professionals want the volunteers to publicly sponsor the organization's policies and programs, and to press for their support. They value having the volunteers get full credit for the organization's achievements, no matter how greatly the professionals have shared in making them possible. The professionals accept the fact that recognition of their own leadership, abilities, and accomplishments does not depend solely nor primarily on their prominence as the spokesmen and advocates for the organization. The professionals who are held in the highest regard are esteemed especially because of their development of the highest quality in volunteer leaders, while infusing the organization with their own expertise, vision, and wisdom. They agree that "there is no limit to what people can do, nor where they can go, if they don't mind who gets the credit."

Successful professionals want to have the volunteers personify the organization. They understand that the prestige of the organization is enhanced by the respect for its leaders, by the confidence and trust in them.

In contrast, organizations marked by confusion or misconceptions regarding the roles, authority, responsibilities, and relationships of volunteers and professionals often struggle with frustration, conflict, and failure to resolve issues. Their internal controversies have sometimes led to the resignation or dismissal of entire staffs, and to the alienation and withdrawal of volunteers.

Because of the necessity for a full partnership between volunteers and professionals, the first priority of outstanding CPOs, when they undertake their responsibility in an organization, is to meet individually with the foremost leaders. The purpose is to learn from both volunteers and professionals their primary interests, concerns, and goals; to obtain their guidance; and to plan how they can work together most effectively. These consultations continue and deepen as an indispensable foundation of their work.

If an organization has suffered from weak volunteers, the new CPO sets as his first priority the rebuilding of volunteer leadership. Striking examples of how critical this is readily come to mind. One organization's previous chief volunteer officer (CVO) and CPO both had been in poor health, and the organization had suffered erosion of its services and support, fragmentation, and disaffection, resulting in discouragement and a loss of morale among volunteers and staff. Before accepting the appointment, the new CPO obtained the commitment of the volunteer leaders that they would renew their involvement. For his part, the CPO committed himself to seek out and involve additional exceptionally able volunteers, who could help reenergize the organization and bring it to new heights. He cautioned that it would take up to six years to achieve this goal, and it did. But by that time the organization had an almost entirely new group of officers and many new board members who strengthened the organization beyond what it had been before the downslide.

Another organization, highly respected for the excellence of its service, its renowned volunteer leaders, and its very able CPO and staff, went into a drastic decline after the CPO retired and was followed by a new CPO who did not involve the volunteers as intensively, did not continue the recruitment and development of other top-grade volunteers, and did not continue to build a quality staff. The partnership of the volunteers and professionals eroded, and the organization sank into mediocrity.

The relationship between the chief volunteer officer and the chief professional officer is crucial. They share the highest responsibilities and leadership of the organization. They work in very close, sometimes daily, consultation and collaboration.

The strength of the relationship is underpinned by principles and guidelines that characterize the leading nonprofit organizations. Carrying them out, however, requires repeated adjustments, tailored to each organization and to the makeup of each pair of CVO and CPO. Each CVO serves in that office for a limited term, usually three to four years. The CPO may continue through a succession of CVOs. Each CVO has a different personality, experience, strengths, and priorities. Each has different work patterns; some are meticulous in focusing on details of the organization's work, while others concentrate on broad concepts and basic goals.

The CPOs in leading organizations are prepared in advance for the changes entailed as a new CVO comes aboard. They know what to expect in the characteristics of the new CVOs, having worked with the new person in his or her previous responsibilities within the organization. The new CVOs usually have held other offices, chaired committees, and performed other services as they advance up the ladder of increasing responsibilities.

Nevertheless, the role of CVO is different from any previous responsibility. To assure a full mutual understanding of how they can team most cooperatively, CVOs and CPOs should begin that partnership by meeting together to clearly define their respective authority and responsibilities, and to outline the procedures by which they can work together most harmoniously and effectively. They also should decide how they will resolve differences between them on any issue.

They understand that the CPOs are responsible to the governing body. That body appointed them, and only it can discharge them. They are agreed that the CPO is not an employee of the CVO. The CPO reports to the CVO, but is responsible to the collective total board.

The CVO and CPO can reconcile any differences they may have regarding the substance of an issue and how to handle it before it is considered by the governing body.

The CPO is evaluated periodically by the governing body or by a subgroup designated by that body, not by the CVO alone.

The CVO understands that the CPO has the responsibility and authority for selecting the remainder of the staff. The CPO may consult with appropriate volunteers in selection of the staff to fill particular positions. The CVO brings suggestions, questions, and criticisms regarding the work of any staff member to the CPO, not to the staff member directly.

> EXAMPLE:
> The CPO of a major organization meets with each newly elected CVO to discuss how they can work together most cooperatively and effectively. They share and discuss their understanding of their respective roles, responsibilities, authority, and accountability, to make sure that they are in full agreement on them.

They consider how they will handle any disagreements they may have on important issues, how they can resolve their differences before the issues are deliberated by the board, and what they will do in the unlikely but possible event that they cannot come to personal agreement.

This organization has been notable for the outstanding collaboration of its CVOs and CPO.

> EXAMPLE:
> A CPO complained about the problems he was having with the CVO. The CVO was the chief executive officer of a very profitable business that he directed with firm authority. He assumed that he had the same authority and responsibility as CVO of the nonprofit organization.

The CPO struggled with the dilemmas created by the CVO's unilateral decisions and directives, unsuccessful relationships, and other confusions. He had not met with the CVO initially to work out a mutual understanding of their respective roles, as the CPO in the previous example had done.

> EXAMPLE:
> Another organization was having problems
> with the confused roles of the CVO and CPO.
> In making a thorough review of its
> governance, the organization found that its
> bylaws identified the CVO as the chief
> executive officer; this was responsible in part
> for the difficulties.

The organization revised its bylaws to remove the term "chief executive officer" and to specify the respective roles of the CVO and CPO. It made clear that the CPO was employed by the board and was primarily accountable to the board, and that the relationship of the CVO and CPO was based on that accountability.

In the leading nonprofits, the CPO and CVO understand that one of their most important responsibilities is to assure succession of the CVO by the strongest, most influential leader. They join in identifying the best candidates, and in preparing them for election to the highest office as they advance through a series of increasing responsibilities. When the CVO's term of office ends and the choice of a successor must be made, there should be at least two or more persons qualified and recognized as deserving the honor and responsibility because of the exceptional service they have rendered.

The principles and procedures that characterize the relationship between key volunteers and professionals in leading nonprofit organizations are applied to all volunteers and staff. Mutual understanding is developed as a primary element in the training of both. The CVOs and officers work to assure it in their continuing guidance of the volunteers; the CPOs and their executive associates continue to monitor and deepen it in the staff.

In performing the services that carry out the purposes and functions of the organization, the professionals work under the oversight of volunteers, usually through committees. This oversight provides the organization with the benefit of advice from the volunteers and allows it to ascertain that the staff adheres to the policies, programs, and financing determined by the governing bodies; oversight confirms that the organization's implementation of its goals is as effective and economical as possible. The purpose of the oversight is to detect any deviations or shortcomings, to help correct them, and to learn of any failures and how they can be overcome, so that the programs can be modified, replaced, or discarded if necessary. The volunteers are charged with the responsibility to be alert to unforeseen changes in circumstances, needs, scientific knowledge, and opportunities that may require revisions or new initiatives in the organization's services.

Concurrently, the CPOs deepen the understanding and skills of their staffs in how to work most closely, cooperatively, and productively with volunteers. CPOs have frequently found that professionals who may be highly expert in the substance of their work were never trained in the special relationship of volunteers and staffs. Outstanding CPOs recognize that this relationship is crucial to an organization's success. The required understanding is developed as a central element of the ongoing supervision, guidance, and evaluation of the staff.

6

———··◆··———

FINANCE

Just as human resources are the heart of nonprofit organizations, financial resources are the lifeblood. Their finances make possible how much they can do, and how well they can do it.

Service organizations rarely have enough money to meet all of the needs they are trying to overcome. And because of inflation and rising costs of goods and services, they must raise more just to stand still. We will focus here on the organizations that are primarily responsible for raising their funds. Others are financed by federations, of which they are beneficiaries, or are foundations that are endowed and that receive allocated funds from the annual earnings of their investments. But foundations too may find this analysis and these guides helpful in building their understanding of the self-financing organizations.

The organizations that must obtain their financial support draw sustenance from several components of income—fund raising, government grants, and fees for service, all of which are related parts of financial planning and programs. They are correlated so that each element adds to the others.

Fund Raising

The leading organizations know that they can improve their fund raising—how they organize it, how they apply it. They know that there are potential resources for greater support than they have exploited, from resources they have solicited and from others they have not yet tapped. No organization has reached perfection in this area.

Many valuable books have been written on effective fund raising, and the number grows year by year. The purpose here is not to summarize all that they teach. Rather it is to focus on practices that have proved to be especially valuable for producing greater funds.

Before embarking on their annual fund raising, the leaders of successful organizations plan and budget their operations, and assess their fund-raising potential to determine how much they should try to raise. They weigh the needs of the organization and choose the ones that are most important to finance. They design the services to address those needs. They assure themselves that they have volunteers and staff with the ability to carry out the programs. They determine the costs.

Needs can rarely be met in one year. They require multi-year services. New programs, especially, are likely to grow as they are phased in and developed. Leading organizations take into account what they are committing themselves to, not only in the year ahead but in the years thereafter.

Before attempting to obtain greater funds, they examine whether costs for some ongoing services can be reduced to make way for the new programs, and whether they can cut back services that have achieved their purposes or that may not be as important now as the proposed ones.

They assess their ability to raise the funds, taking into account both internal and external factors. Internally, they analyze whether they have volunteers and staff who are capable of securing the funds, and whether these people have the necessary organization and expertise and the time required in view of other commitments. Externally, they appraise the economy, political changes, and other elements that might have an impact on their financing.

Prior planning and budgeting is the bedrock on which fund raising is based. The process involves men and women who lead by the level of their own gifts and by obtaining the contributions of others. The decision to conduct the programs and to secure the funds is theirs. It verifies their understanding and conviction regarding the importance of the needs and services. It demonstrates the commitment of their own support and underlies their determination to obtain the maximum support of others.

Underpinning the determination of volunteers are staff members who are expert in fund raising. In very small organizations, it is the CPO and possibly others. In larger organizations, it is trained, experienced, and skilled fundraising specialists, in addition to the CPO. These specialists know the most effective strategies and practices, and how to apply them skillfully.

In a number of organizations, fund raising is mapped out by a finance committee that works with the staff through the year. The governing board gives major consideration to the committee's analyses and recommendations, modifying or simply approving them, before authorizing the fund raising.

Financial planning should be comprehensive, taking into account all potential applicable resources, especially individual contributions, planned giving, foundations, corporations, government grants, and fees for service.

Successful organizations select those resources that are most appropriate and feasible for them. While they set fund-raising goals that are "stretch goals"—sums that are obtainable with the utmost effort—they avoid impossible goals that are completely unrealistic. They also avoid "safe" goals that are so modest or minimal that their attainment would mask failure as "success."

They budget their fund-raising costs, setting them at levels that are a minor percentage of income.

Annual Campaigns

Fund-raising campaigns have an organized structure. Volunteers and staff members know what their responsibilities are, and to whom they are accountable. They are supervised to make sure that they fully carry out their responsibilities. Timetables are set for each phase of the fund raising, with target dates for completion so that they do not drag on endlessly. Progress is monitored so that adjustments and corrections can be made without waiting for final results. Outstanding achievements by volunteers are honored in the course of the fund raising, to reward them, to encourage them further, and to stimulate others.

Campaigns for individual gifts begin with the contributions of the members of the governing bodies, who know intimately the importance of the needs and of the services provided. The gifts of these individuals set the standard for others. They understand that unless their gifts are commensurate with the goals, others will not take the goals seriously. Having made example-setting contributions, the board members can then solicit others with credibility.

Another initial priority is the gifts of other volunteers. Their contributions too are standard-setting gifts, typically averaging almost double the gifts of other donors.

In soliciting other prospects, the organizations concentrate on large gifts. A single solicitation by a volunteer to obtain a gift of $5,000 is more productive than twenty-five solicitations to obtain gifts of $25 each. Efforts to obtain $25 gifts should not be slighted, but the focus should be on the greatest potential.

Volunteer workers are solicitors, rather than collectors. They have been trained in how to explain the organization's needs, how to answer questions, how to respond to complaints, and how to overcome resistance. They do not always accept an amount that is initially offered, if inadequate; rather they try to obtain larger contributions, courteously and without offense.

An enshrined fund-raising maxim is that primarily "people give to people, rather than to causes." It has been demonstrated repeatedly that a solicitor who is a friend of the prospect can obtain a generous gift; a solicitor for the same organization who is a stranger to a prospect may obtain a much smaller gift or no contribution at all. Wherever possible, solicitors should be assigned to prospects whom they know and to whom they have ready access.

For major gifts especially, solicitors should meet personally with each prospect and solicit face to face, attempting to obtain amounts that have been suggested by the campaign committees. It has also been demonstrated that for many prospects the most important determinant of how much they give is the example set by the contributions already made by their economic and social peers. Solicitors are therefore assigned to prospects who are their peers, and who can talk to the prospect in terms of the level of their own gifts, which they have already made.

Studies have shown that contributors who have given far less than they could afford often have never been asked for more, and that the reason many people have not contributed to an organization is that they were never asked to give. The leading organizations therefore have redoubled their efforts to solicit people they have never contacted before, and to request larger gifts from people they believe can contribute more than they have in the past.

Successful organizations do not confuse fund raising with public relations. They understand that public relations and public education can help build a readiness to give, and to give more. But they know that the gifts will not be made unless they are obtained by individual solicitations.

Contributors are warmly thanked by the organization for their gifts. For major contributors, especially, the expression of gratitude should be individualized and not a mechanized, impersonal gesture. And organizations should express their deepest appreciation to volunteers who have secured gifts, honoring them individually and publicly.

Between annual campaigns, contributors are kept informed about what their gifts are achieving. The organizations thus work to deepen the interest and understanding of their supporters, to strengthen the basis for continued and greater giving. They reinforce the givers' awareness of how important their assistance is and the great value that is attached to them as contributors.

Endowments

In addition to the quest for annual contributions to finance their ongoing services, in recent years leading voluntary organizations have intensified their efforts to develop endowment funds. They are building their endowment funds to reach a sum based on the organization's thoughtful determination of why it needs such funds and how much endowment should be sought.

Endowments are different in many respects from operating funds. The principal is invested, and usually only the income from the investment is spent. The types of investments are specified by the organization's governing body to avoid speculative risks. Investments are managed by an investment committee and guided by expert investment companies or professionals.

Endowment funds are contributed to an organization for purposes other than ongoing services. The rationale for endowment funds is usually that they will enable the organization to meet emergencies and fund-raising shortfalls, to initiate and test innovative services, to carry out transitions from previous levels of service to new ones, to conduct research, and to undertake time-limited special projects.

Solicitation to obtain endowment contributions also differs from the securing of annual operating funds. While inviting gifts from all, this effort concentrates on individuals and families who have potential to make large contributions. The donors may give the organizations a free hand in allocating the funds, which the organizations prefer, or may restrict their use to specific, named purposes.

Planned giving involves estate planning and tax considerations. Donors can choose from a variety of options for the form of gifts. They may be bequests, trusts, pooled income funds, insurance policies with an organization as the beneficiary, and other alternatives. A donor's gift may be segregated as a "philanthropic fund" maintained as a distinct entity named for the donor, and with the donors able to recommend to the organization the specific grants to be made from their funds.

Donors may set up "supporting foundations" of the organization, usually with substantial funds. Each "supporting foundation" is a separate corporation governed by a board. The majority of the board members are named by the organization, a minority by the donor. The organization thus has final control, but the donor has a strong voice in deciding the management of the foundation and the allocation of funds. These public foundations are not subject to the several governmental regulations that apply to private foundations, and they have the benefits of the expertise of the donee organizations for the management of the funds.

The solicitation and management of planned giving is made by an advisory committee of knowledgeable volunteers and by trained staff members. Each solicitation may require several consultations, over periods of months or even years. Legal advice will usually be sought by the donor and the organization.

Foundations and Corporations

A third important fund-raising resource for voluntary service organizations is foundations and corporations. Organizations are continually alert to the availability of such support for special, time-limited needs—to initiate, test, and demonstrate new programs, to revise services, to conduct research and evaluations, to upgrade services, and to carry out particular projects.

The organizations research the foundations to learn which ones are concerned with the organizations' purposes and fields of service, the types of grants they make and in what amounts, their application and decision-making procedures, and the makeup of their governing boards and staffs.

The same kind of attention is given to corporations that are potential donors. In addition, a growing number of voluntary organizations have responded to the availability of "gifts in kind" by corporations, which donate their products and lend their personnel for management or for application of their particular knowledge and skills.

Government Grants

Another major resource for income is grants—from federal, state, and local governments. For institutions such as hospitals, government is the major source of support.

The leading organizations keep informed of the vast variety of government grants that are available, and of the changes legislated each year that open new opportunities. But they do not automatically apply. They carefully assess the advantage and disadvantage of each potential grant, taking a number of considerations into account. They make sure that the government's purposes for the funds accord with the organization's purposes. They avoid having government funds inadvertently change their priorities. They consider the demands the administration of the government funds will impose on the volunteers' and staff members' energies and time. They assess the overhead costs that may not be covered by the government's administrative allowances in the grants. They give full weight to the heavy reporting and accountability requirements.

When successful organizations apply for government money, it is not a blind chase. Rather it is a planned decision based on all of the considerations; it is knowledgeably undertaken and ably carried out. If leading organizations apply for grants, they do so skillfully.

Fees for Service

Another financial resource, and a growing one, is income from fees for services. Voluntary agencies serve all income levels of the population. Museums, theaters, and family-counseling, child-care, health, geriatric, educational, and other institutions serve many people who are able to pay in whole or in part for services they receive.

The leading organizations routinely review their fee-payment policies and practices. They adjust to the current realities of costs, making changes required by inflation and other developments. One motivation, in addition to the pressing need for the income, is the realization that when people pay for services they receive, they are verifying the importance and value they attach to the service. At the same time, the organizations try to make sure that they do not deny services to people who need them but who cannot afford to pay for them.

Capital Funds

The leading nonprofit organizations have also been fine-tuning their fund raising for capital purposes—for buildings, equipment, and other requirements. They analyze in depth whether they must have the additions and what the alternatives might be; the realistic costs, bearing in mind the many cases in which costs have outrun projections; the timetables for completing the construction or obtaining the equipment, again considering the many cases of long delays beyond original commitments and expectations.

They do not build an additional facility simply because a donor offers to make an extraordinary gift to construct or obtain it—no matter how attractive the amount of the contribution, or the prestige of the donor—if the addition is not needed, if its purpose or function would be outside the scope of the organization, or if it is less important than other requirements.

They research and appraise designs and expectations, having witnessed examples of misfit architecture, ill-designed facilities, and disappointing equipment. They obtain the best experts that they can get to guide them. They refuse to be trapped into employing architects, builders, contractors, and suppliers whose "qualifications" are that they are friends of officers or board members.

The leading organizations have been disciplined in calculating the funds not only for construction and acquisition, but also for future maintenance costs and the costs of the services for which the additions are built; such considerations are critical. Before committing themselves to the capital venture, successful organizations insist that these greater operating costs be financed.

In planning their comprehensive financing, the leading organizations consider the many external elements that may have an impact on what they can obtain. They assess the economic, political, and social conditions, and the fund raising of competitive organizations. They appraise the optimism or pessimism of people regarding the immediate economic future, knowing that these psychological expectations often affect people's decisions more than current conditions.

They give special attention to government tax laws that encourage or depress how much people contribute. They are especially sensitive to this, having experienced the effects of the 1986 federal tax changes, which caused sharp losses in gifts from the wealthiest contributors.

The leading organizations have mobilized themselves to act more aggressively and cohesively, in joint efforts and in a directed fashion, to obtain legislation that will encourage contributions; to defeat proposed laws or remove existing legislation that inhibits giving and reduces contributions; to support legislation that will enlarge government grants to voluntary organizations for vital services; and to oppose cuts in grants that shrink or cripple their services.

7

CHANGE

In a world and society that are undergoing the most rapid changes in all history—changes that have an impact on the needs that nonprofits address and the services they perform—the leading organizations know that change is inevitable in what they do and how they do it. They are alert and sensitive to what is happening and to what may be likely to happen, and they adjust their services as quickly as possible.

The strongest nonprofit organizations are not satisfied with what they have achieved. They are well aware that no organization has achieved perfection. There is always room for improvement. They have an unceasing creative discontent.

These organizations are continually concerned with whether they are doing what is most important, and whether they are doing it as well as they might. They are sensitive to the reality that what has been most significant in the past may no longer be as relevant, and that what has been the highest quality may now be second-best because of advances in knowledge and skills.

They are alert to new opportunities, conditions, and resources, to the innovations of others that they can replicate or adapt and that enable them to achieve what they could not accomplish before. They are wary of drifting into obsolescence. The organizations are not only reactors, they are initiators and innovators.

The leading organizations continuously evaluate their goals, priorities, and programs; in this ongoing process, each service may be revised, if warranted. Periodically they make comprehensive reviews of their overall goals, priorities, services, finances, and administration.

There are many pressures for change, from a variety of sources. Staff members and volunteers are on the front line of confronting the needs. They learn which services are productive and which are not achieving their purposes. Members of the board, committees, and constituency may press the organization to tackle new or neglected problems. Changing government policies and funding may force the organization to change. Other pressures may come from the media, events such as crimes in the area, from deaths that could have been prevented, or from the pleas of special interest groups. The pressures underscore that "what logic may not persuade, necessity may command."

When confronted with the challenges to change, the leaders and staffs of the strongest organizations do not have an automatic knee-jerk reaction of "We can't do that—it's not the way we have done things." Rather they ask "Why not?"

Instead of resisting the challenges, they welcome them, to reconsider what they do, to see if they can do better, to adapt, extend, and enrich what they perform. They are aware that the new service need not always displace ones already in place; instead it may augment and improve them.

But the obstacles to change are deeply imbedded and difficult to overcome. What is already in place may be viewed as sacred. Governing bodies and professional staffs may be reluctant to give up current practices or to alter them. They do not want to discard the known for the untested. Individual members of boards and staffs may have different values and standards. The gap between what exists and what could be may be intolerable to some, but not a problem to others. Some may fear, consciously or unconsciously, that added services will bring into the organization new people in governance to displace them from the authority and responsibility they cherish. The leading organizations are very sensitive to these fears; they understand that distrust and resistance may have to be overcome in order to make changes.

Organizations differ on how they achieve change, depending on their history, composition, the community in which they serve, and other factors.

Change should not occur only for the sake of change. The revision must be justified by assurance that it will enable the organizations to achieve more.

Flexibility is balanced by stability. Any change should not disrupt the organization's ability to carry out its total responsibilities most effectively. Changes must be timed so that the organization is able to apply them constructively, and they must be planned, deliberately and in an orderly fashion. They should be accompanied by measures that retain the commitment of the organization's leaders, constituents, and staff.

In leading organizations, changes are undertaken with realistic expectations. The organizations are aware that most advances are incremental, not immediately tremendous or sensational. Each advance is a building block, erected on what has been achieved; on each new block, in turn, further gains can be based, in an ever-growing advancement. Successful organizations have a vision of the entire structure, not only of each block.

The best organizations seek genuine improvements, not an alteration of their image. They distinguish between movement that goes forward, and motion on a stationary treadmill. Their readiness to change is part of their unceasing search for authentic better service, with genuine greater achievement.

8

PLANNING AND BUDGETING

Leading nonprofits define their priorities. They concentrate on the needs and services that are central to their purposes and mission. They set annual and long-term goals, monitor their work to accord with these goals, and analyze how fully they have achieved them. Consideration of each proposed new, additional, or revised service is related to the overall goals and priorities, and is assessed in terms of the effect it will have on existing services and whether the organization has the capacity to perform it effectively.

In contrast, other organizations often take on responsibilities in reaction to each pressure. They then struggle with inadequate funds to finance the new services. Their staffs are spread thin, struggling to keep their heads above water. There is no defined order of priorities.

The planning that is done by leading nonprofits is proactive. The organizations are alert to changing needs and opportunities. They try to address problems in their early stages, when they can be handled more successfully and at less cost than when they become emergencies or crises. They seek to prevent problems, knowing that the human and dollar cost of prevention is far less than the cost of overcoming damage after it has happened.

Much planning is ongoing, stimulated by and built on the continuing insights gained by staff members and volunteers from their work, from their creativity, and from the pressures of events. Planning is intrinsic to the supervisory conferences of executives and staff members, staff group discussions, volunteer committees, and governing board meetings.

Planning is linked to budgeting and financing. Planning that does not take full account of costs, and of the realities of obtaining the required funds, is a fruitless exercise. Individuals named as planners should be among the strongest leaders of an organization, people with the ability to influence others and carry out what they project. They also should be the people most vitally concerned with particular issues. They should share fully in the analysis of the problem or project, and in concluding whether action should be taken and, if so, what action.

Such a planning process assures that what is projected will be carried out. It is not theoretical. It results in action.

Planning should be both short-range and long-range. Problems and needs can seldom be overcome or substantially alleviated in one year. Multi-year programs and cost projections are required. New services seldom start full-fledged in the first year. They generally have to be phased in and incrementally developed year by year. Successful plans forecast the expected level to be reached each year, with a cost estimate for each stage.

The focus of good planning is not primarily on institutions, but on people and their needs, and on the services necessary to respond to these needs. The goal is to improve the quality of life of individuals, families, neighborhoods, and communities. The institution is the means to an end, not an end in itself.

In addition to their ongoing planning, the leading organizations often undertake specific planning processes to address particular issues. In this disciplined procedure, the issues to be addressed are carefully defined. The planning concentrates on them and does not stray into unrelated concerns.

Proper planning is done in depth. It distinguishes causes from symptoms, and concentrates on causes. It is comprehensive. Organizations understand that problems are seldom one-dimensional. Successful planners attempt to identify each element, understand it, and relate it to the other elements. They concretize the issues and avoid amorphous generalities and abstractions.

Effective planning—and later evaluations—avoid undefined characterizations. Instead of depicting a situation simply as "bad" or "good," planners make clear what is meant by "bad" or "good," and why it is "bad" or "good." Instead of describing a service as "successful," they spell out what is meant by "success." Instead of words like "a high proportion" or "many" or "few," they specify what is meant by each term.

The need for such planning is not always automatically understood or endorsed by everyone, even in advanced organizations. Especially in addressing new issues, there can be resistance from people who say, "We know the problem;

we know the solution; let's not waste time on planning. Let's get the money and go to work." Such people have to be convinced that others who share the responsibility for decisions and who are equally concerned do not agree that they have all the necessary facts, and may have other views about the problems and what should be done about them; and that the organization cannot act without taking account of these differences, it must resolve them. Opponents of planning have to be assured that they will have a full opportunity to convince the others, while listening to those who differ from them.

Differences in approaches to planning are often rooted in underlying attitudes. In some cases, the problem may be the proverbial distinction between whether the glass is half empty or half full. What may be distressful to some may not be considered a problem by others. Issues that some feel must be addressed, others believe can be ignored. In other instances, what some view as unwelcome aggravations, others see as opportunities to build upon. What some resist facing, others view as a new opening for the resolution of problems and the achievement of goals. The leading organizations expect resistance to planning, prepare for it, and work skillfully to prevent or overcome it.

Planning is applied not only to what is to be done and how it should be done, but also to how well it is to be done. In many cases, a required excellence of performance may be the primary motivation for planning. The best leaders do not tolerate mediocrity, considering it an injustice to the people served and to the organization that serves. They consider it a grievous obstacle to accomplishing what could be achieved, to resolving problems that could be overcome or greatly alleviated.

In setting their priorities, the leading organizations define the goals most vital in carrying out their mission and the services to achieve those goals. Their concentration is motivated by principle and by necessity. They put their funds and energies into what will accomplish the most for their purposes. The focus that is part of their planning is compelled by the realistic view that no organization has enough funds to do everything demanded of it, and must identify and do what is most vital.

That identification is guided by formulated criteria that characteristically include: what services will accomplish most for the most important needs and goals; what the organization is most capable of performing; the required sequence of actions—what must be done first before other steps can be taken; the magnitude of the pressures to undertake a service; and, underlying them all, the values that are the foundation of the organization.

Budgeting

Planning and budgeting are interdependent. The best budgeting is concerned with what should be done in the future, and is not shackled by what has been done in the past. Programs have to justify their costs by what they may achieve in the future, not only by what they have already achieved.

Budgeting is functional. It is not only a listing of salaries, rent, telephone, mail, and other such items; it also relates to programs and services. The expense of each service is related to the cost of other services. In making budgetary calculations, successful organizations understand that the cost of each function is not necessarily proportionate to its priority. The most vital services are not always the most costly.

The organizations understand, too, that their budgets must have credibility. Expense and income are balanced.

Prospective increases in costs are matched by prospective authentic increases in income.

Good budgets are not only meticulously prepared, they are scrupulously carried out. Expenditures are controlled to match actual income. Scheduled analyses, monthly or at other intervals, enable the CVO and staff responsible for finances to identify deviations quickly, and to take the actions necessary to prevent deficits.

Research

Essential for both planning and budgeting is increasingly refined research, which is ongoing in an organization's operation, and extends to special studies of particular issues. Research provides information and analyses the organization needs to understand, in depth, the problems and issues being addressed, their causes, their component elements, related services, and their results. It identifies unmet needs and helps to clarify pros and cons of alternative options, costs, and other factors. It is pragmatic research, tailored to the needs of each organization. It is applied research; it is used.

Organizations, small as well as large, have computerized their record keeping and have compiled data banks on which they can draw to obtain the facts they must have to administer their programs, evaluate what they do, and draw implications for future policies and services.

In undertaking special studies, the organizations may engage specialists to provide the expertise, objectivity, and integrity that will make the findings unassailable.

The ingredients of research are seldom only quantitative. Much of the research may be qualitative, involving attitudes, values, and relationships. People with strong views on issues readily search for evidence of bias and incompleteness, particularly when the findings of the research are not to their liking. When it is unassailable, high-quality research can help build a greater depth of understanding that can expedite consensus decisions.

In employing outside experts to conduct special studies, leading organizations have found it essential to precisely define the responsibilities of the experts. They assure that the experts present, without compromise, the facts and analyses that emerge from the research; they also assure that they will not go beyond their competence and mandate. Good researchers limit their reports to the findings of the research. They do not go beyond them to offer views on an organization's policies and services, which must take account of many other elements that the researchers have not dealt with and may not understand. I have seen excellent factual studies and analyses ruined by researchers who went beyond their findings to make recommendations that undermined the credibility of their work overall.

The best organizations regard the involvement of volunteer leaders and staff members in research as essential to assure that findings will be used in arriving at decisions and implementing them. Both volunteers and professionals participate from the very beginning of the process in determining to undertake the research, in defining its purposes, and in assessing and applying what comes out of it. They authorize and structure the research so that it will expedite sound decisions and actions, and they guard against having it used to needlessly delay action or substitute for action.

Volunteers and staff are continuously involved in the research. They receive progress reports, where appropriate and feasible as the research progresses, so that they can learn from it, can assess its focus and adequacy, and can help guide next steps and redirect it if they find it has gone off track.

Good researchers test preliminary findings with volunteers and staff, seeking their input before reports are finalized. Research is a working tool in an organization's planning process. It deepens the organization's understanding as it proceeds. The ongoing involvement of volunteers and staff members minimizes the likelihood of surprise when findings are announced, and expedites the readiness to deal with them. It builds confidence in what has been done and what is revealed, and strengthens the readiness to apply what has been learned.

9

---···◆·◆·◆···---

INVOLVEMENT

Volunteers are intensively involved in governing the leading nonprofit organizations. They determine their policies. They implement them. They select and authorize the organizations' services and oversee their administration.

The volunteers participate actively in every stage of developing and making decisions. They can support the decisions, can defend them if challenged, and are accountable for them.

Intensive involvement not only firmly underpins the decision on a particular issue; it strengthens the organization itself. It enlarges the capacity of the organization to handle other future issues successfully, sharpens the skills to deal with them, cements the relationship of diverse people in working together to achieve consensus, and deepens the commitment of the volunteers to the organization. The procedure for processing each issue is planned with these larger goals in mind.

Gains are achieved not only by a final decision and its implementation. Advances are made in the very process of formulating decisions. The volunteers' understanding, views, and relationships change as the deliberations proceed. Programs are revised, when such a need is clearly indicated, without waiting for the conclusion of the process.

So impressively have such gains been demonstrated that it has often been said that "the process is the product." The process is in fact an indispensable and vital part of the product, but it is not the entire product. The full product is the final decision and its implementation.

The intensive involvement of volunteers gives them a sense of "ownership" of the organization and their actions. It is their organization, just as citizens in a democracy "own" their government. It is their instrument; they shape its policies, mandate its programs, and determine its finances.

A vivid example of what to do and what not to do occurred in two neighboring communities where similar organizations addressed parallel concerns at the same time. The executive of one organization drew up a master plan that defined every element of proposed changes in the scope, responsibilities, and structure of his organization, specifying the revised composition of its governing board, committees, departments and staff, and financing. He then presented the blueprint to his board.

The other community organization appointed a committee composed of leaders with a diversity of views and relationships. The committee first defined the questions to be addressed and the process that would attempt to find the answers. The next step was to obtain the experience of other communities that had acted on similar concerns. The third step was to convene a series of "town meetings" of leaders of the various segments of the community that would be affected by the decisions. The size of each meeting was limited in order to make possible active participation in the discussions by all present.

No proposed solutions were brought by the committee to these meetings. Rather the participants were asked for their judgments on the problems, their analyses of the causes, and whether they thought anything should be done about them other than what was already under way and, if so, what.

The views and proposals that emerged from these meetings, together with what was learned from experience elsewhere, were assessed by the committee. Its members added their own judgments and crystallized recommendations of what appeared to be the best wisdom and the most desirable and realistic course of action. The committee's formulation was then tested in further "town meetings" with the leaders who had been consulted previously. When a consensus was developed, the recommendations were presented to the governing body of the sponsoring organization, which had been kept informed and consulted throughout the process. The recommendations for major changes were approved and implemented.

This step-by-step process consumed about a year. In contrast, the "shortcut" of the first community, limited to the blueprint developed and presented by the professional executive virtually alone, was never approved. It died in the board.

The people involved in the governance of leading voluntary organizations are the volunteers most concerned with the mission of the organizations and their needs and services. They are the people whose knowledge, experience, and judgment can best strengthen what the organization does and build its capacity to achieve; whose support for the organization's decisions and actions is essential for their success; who can obtain the support of others for the organization.

Successful organizations involve leaders who have followers, people who have the esteem, ability, and relationships to accomplish what they undertake. Organizations are judged not only by their purposes and programs, but by the quality of volunteers who lead them. The involvement of the most respected people, in itself, builds commitment to the organizations.

Struggling organizations often make the mistake of not trying to involve the top rung of leaders because "they are too busy and wouldn't accept." To their dismay, such organizations have seen other organizations reach out to such leaders and enroll them. Leading organizations do not assume that the ablest people will refuse responsibility; they cultivate these leaders and work to obtain them. If what the organization does is important, and if these outstanding men and women are approached by the "right person in the right way" (to be described below), they often come aboard.

Leading organizations engage the most influential volunteers not only for the strengths they bring, but also to safeguard against the harm some might do, often unintentionally, if they are not involved. When uninvolved and uninformed, such people can unwittingly take positions and advocate programs that obstruct or even set back the work of an organization.

The best organizations are careful to tailor the utilization of outstanding leaders to their interests and time. They do not give the busiest, most influential volunteers menial tasks. The meetings they are asked to attend have important agendas, consider serious concerns, and act.

If some of the people being sought are already committed to other responsibilities that will not permit their serving continuously on a governing board, an organization can try to involve them in a time-limited committee or task force on a specific issue, or can attempt to consult with them individually to obtain their judgment and advice.

The involvement of such influential people should not be done at the price of excluding others. Leading organizations are not monolithic or elitist. They are careful to include a cross section of their constituencies, people with a comprehensive range of experience and views that enrich the substance of their deliberations, and whose diversity adds spice and liveliness to discussions.

The organizations are fully aware that people deeply concerned with an issue or problem insist on having decisions made with them, not for them. They want to be part of the decision making from the beginning of the process, not brought in at a later stage as a "second team."

The organizations make a point of including volunteers who may differ greatly on what the priorities and policies of the organizations should be, and on the solutions for specific problems. However, their inclusion makes them "insiders" instead of "outsiders." No matter how greatly they may then disagree with a decision, they cannot claim that they have not been heard, that they did not have a full opportunity to convince others before the decisions were made.

They are involved in every step of the process to develop the conclusions. They may or may not convince others to accept their positions. They may or may not be persuaded by others to change their own views. But often changes do take place, with mutual adjustments and compromises, and agreements are reached that all or virtually all can support. The result is not only the specific action made possible, but a stronger, more unified organization, rather than one fragmented by disaffection.

Not all people with power and influence are calm, reasoned, informed, and logical. Some are emotional, resistant to change, and demanding. Volunteer leaders and professional staffs face the reality that such people will not be passive or silent on an issue that deeply concerns them. Successful organizations do not ignore such individuals. They have developed the art and skills to reach out to them and involve them. Knowing what to expect, the volunteers and professionals do not respond with impatience, emotion, irritation, or upset. They do not alienate such people by their own behavior. They focus the discussion on the substance of the issues, not on the personalities. They maintain their good humor. They keep in mind also that, while there may be strong differences on a particular issue, these "difficult" people may agree on other issues and support the organization in resolving them.

Their responses recall Abraham Lincoln's patient and kind treatment of his severest critics. When asked to explain why he didn't destroy his enemies, his comment was, "I do destroy my enemies, when I convert them into my friends."

In contrast, organizations have been blocked from carrying out what they have tried to accomplish because they failed to include in their deliberations the people opposed to the views of their officers. Their volunteer leaders and professional staffs operated on the premise that they had to keep opponents out because they would be too difficult and disruptive in the discussions. The result was frustration and immobility.

EXAMPLE:
A young CPO, in his first executive position with a small, struggling organization, had a

number of creative proposals for overcoming
the organization's immobility that he wanted
the board to consider. The CVO appointed
committees to consider them and bring their
advice to the board.

The committees endorsed the proposals, but each was
rejected by the board because of the opposition of a faction
of members who had not been members of the committees.
The CVO had omitted them because they were consistently
"naysayers."

The CVO's strategy was manifestly a self-defeating failure,
even more because the opponents resented being excluded
from the committees. When it was pointed out by a veteran
CPO that it would have been wiser to place the opponents
on the committees where they could have expressed their
views, listened to others who differed, broadened their understanding, possibly modified their judgments or the judgments of others, and perhaps reached agreement on compromises that the board would then adopt—the CPO fully
agreed.

Leading organizations involve young men and women,
as well as veterans, in working to build a better future. Young
people who feel strongly that it is their future, want to bring
their own perspective, values, and judgment to help shape it.

Some organizations conduct continuing systematic programs to assure that they will have uninterrupted, highest-
quality volunteer leadership. They: identify young men and
women with outstanding potential for leadership; recruit
them; train them in a series of learning sessions on the
organization's missions, services, governance, financing, and
other basic elements; place them on the committees of
greatest interest to them and involve them in other volunteer activities; and give them increasingly important respon-

sibilities to qualify for board membership and possibly to become officers.

The expiration of terms of office in governing bodies, the opening up of new issues and the need for committees or task forces to work on them—these are opportunities to involve additional people. The organizations gain the enrichment of the newcomers' knowledge, experience, fresh views, expertise, and skills.

The identification of whom to involve is the first step. Obtaining their involvement is the second and crucial step. The leading organizations recruit expertly and skillfully. As in fund raising, who recruits each prospect is critical. The recruitment is done primarily by volunteer leaders. Wherever possible, the approaches are made by people who know the prospects personally and are likely to have the greatest influence in obtaining them.

In other cases, the president of the organization or the chairperson of the nominating committee may invite them. The fact that one of the most prestigious leaders of the organization makes the request underscores the importance of the invitation and of the person being approached. People often feel honored by such an invitation.

For the most important choices, the prospect is visited personally when the invitation is extended. For others, the invitation may be extended by telephone. Letters alone are the least-preferred method; they should be used mainly to confirm a visit or telephone call.

Invitations should not be cheapened by the claim that the "responsibility will take only a little of your time." Instead, the importance of the responsibility should be stressed. If it is worth doing, it is worth the time required.

But neither should the involvement be presented as a burdensome chore. What is held out is the gratification and joy it will bring: the pleasure of a meaningful service, highly desired achievement, working with people whose interests and concerns the prospective volunteers share, whom they respect, and with whom they want to be associated.

All newly elected board members should be prepared for their responsibilities by involvement in expertly planned and executed orientation programs. They are provided histories of the organization, mission statements, governing bylaws, explanations of finances and services, the responsibilities of the board and how it functions, and other basic information. They are engaged in orientation sessions with the CVO, the CPO, and other appropriate volunteers and staff. They hear oral presentations, obtain answers to their questions, express their reactions to what they have received, and bring their own views to the organization's leaders.

Successful organizations also carefully involve the constituencies to whom the governing bodies are accountable. They include a cross section of their constituencies in their governing boards. They keep the constituents informed of the issues being confronted, the decisions being made, the actions being taken. They report to their constituencies with credibility, revealing not only the successes but also the shortcomings of the organization. They build a greater understanding of the needs being addressed and of the services being provided.

Where appropriate, an organization may invite the views and guidance of their constituencies, by mail, telephone, and in some instances interviews with a representative sample of individuals. They may submit preliminary conclusions to obtain the reactions of the constituents before making final decisions.

At the same time, prudent organizations are careful not to create false expectations by eliciting the advice of constituents. They make clear that each person's views will be considered, together with the views of others who may differ, and that all must be weighed.

Leading organizations involve other agencies as well as individuals when they consider policies, issues, and actions that will affect other organizations. They consult with the agencies' volunteer leaders and staffs, and may include them in their committees and task forces. They learn from them, share with them, plan with them, thereby building greater mutual understanding and cooperation. If the conclusion of the joint planning is to share responsibilities with other agencies, those agencies will have been fully involved in reaching the decision.

10

COMMITTEES – SOME PRIORITIES

Perhaps no instruments of business, government, and nonprofit organizations have been ridiculed more than committees. The disparaging jokes about them are legion, and many of the committees have deserved them. Countless times people have left committee meetings with one comment: "A waste of time."

But that is not because committees are inherently flawed. It is because some committees have been misused and abused, often because of ineptness, but sometimes because of intent.

Committees in leading nonprofit organizations are productive and indeed indispensable in handling major issues and policy concerns. They obtain and analyze essential facts, develop options for resolving them, weigh the strengths and weaknesses of each alternative, overcome differences, achieve consensus, and bring their findings and recommendations to their boards, making possible thorough consideration and final decision. They provide a concentration and depth that the boards could not match.

Members of such committees serve with satisfaction and pleasure. They feel rewarded for what they have learned, shared, and achieved.

Their committees have met the following tests:

Integrity

They have been created to oversee and guide an aspect of the agency's work or to help resolve a specific problem, seize a new opportunity, or achieve a defined purpose. They have a mandate to work, to accomplish a result. They are not set up as a subterfuge or a ploy to delay action or block it.

Charge

They know their responsibility. They have been given a written charge, defining what they are to address and what type of product they are expected to bring back to the board—whether an analysis of an issue, options for action, or recommendations for a solution. They are given a time deadline to complete their assignment.

Without such a charge, committees can wander into wastelands beyond their mandate and competence, diffusing and confusing what they try to do, misguiding rather than strengthening their organizations, and preventing progress. If they adhere to their charge, committees stay out of the quicksand and can make major gains.

Example:

A committee was set up by two major organizations to explore their future relationships, with the possibility of close cooperation in a number of functions and perhaps a full merger. They had already consolidated a number of activities, including an annual joint fund-raising campaign, with a ten-year agreement on division of the income. A leader of one of the organizations insisted that there should be no merger unless the allocation formula was changed. This was an extremely sensitive issue. The formula had been worked out with intense negotiations to accommodate deep loyalties to each organization. For the committee to try to change it while the agreement had several more years of life would have destroyed any possibility of merger.

The committee chairperson disposed of the problem quickly and automatically without discussion, by reminding the members that the allocation of funds was outside its charge. As the committee had no authority to deal with it, he ruled it out of order. The committee proceeded with its charge and achieved the full merger.

CVO-Appointed Committees

The chief volunteer officer, with the assistance of the staff, appoints the committees. The committee chairperson may be consulted but does not make the selection. The CVO and staff know the human resources of the organization. They know the qualifications, interests, and concerns of the volunteers. They know who would want most to serve and who would resent not being appointed. They take into account the diversity of views to make sure that the full range of differences will be expressed and considered, to be resolved by the committee.

Composition

Thus the committee members are especially qualified for the responsibility. They are not named to the committee because they happen to be friends of the CVO. They have the ability to address the issue intelligently and competently. They have the commitment to invest their time in it, to work at it.

Their diversity enables the members who previously may have discussed the matter only with those who agreed with them to be confronted by other views, held by other people who are just as earnest and who have as much intelligence and conviction. The diversity of composition compels members to try to persuade others to embrace their positions or be convinced by alternate views.

> EXAMPLE:
> In the committee described above that
> adhered to its charge, the diversity ranged
> from persons who urged at the first meeting,
> "If it ain't broke, don't fix it," to those at the
> other extreme who advised, "Let's not beat
> around the bush—let's merge." The differences
> were overcome in the committee process. The
> committee came to the two boards with a
> virtually unanimous recommendation for
> merger. (The steps taken to achieve this are
> described in Chapter Eleven.)

Beyond their particular function, committees help to identify and groom potential future top leaders of the organization. Such individuals are assigned to committees whose responsibilities especially concern them. In the committee experience, they gain a greater understanding of the organization, and more broadly of how nonprofit organizations function, in contrast to their business, professional, or government backgrounds. As they merit advancement, they are moved up to increased responsibilities as vice-chairpersons or chairpersons. In those capacities, they may meet with the chairpersons of other committees to coordinate their work and share in the overall operation of the organization.

Young men and women are included in the committees. Working with veteran members, they feel that the committees will help shape the future of the organization. Young people assert that they have a longer, greater stake in that future. They want a voice in determining it.

Leading organizations welcome the participation of young people, who often bring a different perspective. They contribute understanding and abilities the organizations need. They are a refreshing ingredient. They are laying the groundwork for their advance to greater leadership.

The membership of committees need not be limited to board members. They may include others who can contribute knowledge and influence. They may be people the organization would like to have serve on the board; committee service may help prepare and qualify them for it.

Members of time-limited committees (not standing committees) work as a stable group. They are not repeatedly interrupted and set back by new people joining the committee. The new member would not have been part of the previous discussions, would not have shared in the step-by-step advancement of the process. Latecomers can unwittingly but readily compromise the committee's progress, as they have done in organizations that shift the membership of committees in the course of their work.

Size

Successful committees are not too large to function as a working group. The members can express their views. They can converse actively with the others. The preferred maximum is twenty-five to thirty members if that many are required in order to represent all factions. If larger numbers are needed by some committees or commissions in order to represent all essential parties, they can achieve the necessary participation, dialogue, and depth of analysis and consideration through subcommittees and task forces on particular elements of the charge.

Chairperson

Organizations have found that a "must" for committees is a fully qualified chairperson. How she or he relates to the members, conducts meetings, handles the consideration of opposing positions, guides the discussions, helps develop elements of agreement, and achieves consensus may determine whether the committee succeeds or fails.

In selecting committee chairpersons, leading organizations apply the following criteria, among others:

Chairpersons must have the respect and trust of all members and be acceptable to all factions. They must be open to all views, and must have them considered fairly and fully by the committee.

They must know enough about the issues to handle discussions intelligently.

The subject must be important to them, worth the heavy investment the responsibility requires, including not only conducting the committee meetings, but preparation for each session: telephone calls and meetings with key individual members to clarify their views, attempts to resolve differences, and arranging for committee members to present reports or to speak at meetings.

Chairpersons must have the skills to conduct discussions so that each session advances the committee toward achievement of its goal. They elicit the views of the members. They are able to listen, do not dominate meetings, and refrain from responding personally to every comment.

They distinguish central matters from peripheral ones, and have the committee concentrate on the essence. They astutely identify elements of agreement, define them, and gain full support for them. They clarify points of disagreement, probe the reasons for the differences, and guide members in resolving them. They relate to opposing partisans with courtesy and civility.

A prized quality in a chairperson is a sense of humor. Leaders with that asset are able to dispel heated, adversarial tensions with an artful quip, an apt anecdote, or a pertinent joke; they can elicit bursts of laughter, change heaviness to lightness, and restore amiability.

The chairperson welds what started as mix of individuals into a cordial working group, relating the members to each other with increasingly close bonding.

Staff

Each committee is served by a professional staff member, who has an essential, vital role. How well or poorly the staff member performs often makes the difference between a

productive and an aimless, frustrated committee. Leading organizations assign staff members who are qualified for their committee responsibilities. These people are not only experts in the field of the committee's work; they are also skilled in serving committees. A common cause of failure is that a staff member may be an outstanding specialist in his or her daily work, but inept in working with committees. The professionals must be trained to work with committees. Leading organizations make sure they are.

The professional works with the chairperson to plan the operation of the committee, develop the strategies, and analyze and evaluate the group's ongoing work; he or she provides the information the committee requires and participates in its discussions.

The staff member listens intently at the meetings to assess whether the discussion is focused and disciplined or wanders into peripheral or unrelated byways, and confers with the chairperson to bring it back to essentials.

As needed during meetings, the staff member may provide facts on the matter under consideration in order for the committee to understand the issue and address it intelligently. The information may illuminate what is being considered; may inform about whether the organization has addressed it in the past, and with what result; and may inform the group whether other organizations have already undertaken what is being proposed, so that the committee can learn from their experience.

Staff members are alert to perceive information, judgments, and proposals introduced by committee members during the discussions that had not been anticipated and that could be valuable in advancing the committee's progress. The professional points them out for the committee to consider.

The professional objectively asks penetrating questions of committee members to clarify their positions, and to reveal the strengths and expose the weaknesses of their arguments. Instead of the staff member becoming an opponent or a supporter of a proposition, he or she draws out the advocates so that they strengthen or undermine their arguments with their own responses to the questions. The staff member likewise prompts the chairperson to call upon committee members who have been silent but whose judgments are known to be valuable and influential, and whose participation will advance the committee's progress.

Throughout the deliberations, professional assistance to the chairperson is discreet and unobtrusive, with frequent use of whispered comments and questions.

Like the chairperson, the staff member maintains an objectivity and openness that has the respect and trust of all members. The objectivity and openness are maintained not only in meetings but throughout all elements of the process. Between meetings, in discussions with subgroups or individuals, and in casual conversations where the subject may arise, the staff member is careful to refrain from any remarks that may be disparaging or caustic about committee members and their views.

Failure to observe that caution has caused serious damage. Cynical comments by staff members may offend the listeners, be overheard by others, be spread and magnified, and seriously complicate and obstruct the committee's work.

The staff member makes clear by his or her behavior that decisions will be made genuinely by the volunteer members, based on their judgments, and not as a rubber stamp for the professionals. With that objective in mind, the staff member offers his or her opinions and advice at carefully chosen times when it may be especially needed, to clarify and guide.

The professional understands that the most persuasive force in winning support for a position may be the person who advocates it. The decision often depends on the respect the sponsor commands, and the confidence and faith in his or her judgment and wisdom. The professional and chairperson therefore arrange with well-respected volunteers in advance of meetings to present their views. Even if the professional originated the proposal, it may be more effective to have a committee member who enthusiastically supports it become the initiator and sponsor at the meeting.

At the close of a session, when appropriate, the professional may summarize what the committee has achieved—the most important insights and judgments that have been developed, the agreements reached, the issues not yet resolved, the next steps directed or indicated. Instead of each member leaving with a personal and often differing perception of what took place, which may be fragmented and disjointed, the summary pulls together the elements into a uniform, cohesive understanding among all committee members of the progress that was made and of what will follow.

Meetings

Meetings are scheduled as much as a year in advance. The most important and busiest members quickly fill their calendars with other commitments. In such an environment, the only way to obtain full participation in the committee's work is to schedule it well into the future.

Each meeting is planned, organized, and conducted to achieve a definite purpose. It advances the committee toward its ultimate goal. It satisfies the most demanding and critical members because of its preparation, content, and accomplishment.

The meeting may:

1. Clarify issues as a requirement for resolving them.

2. Identify specific points of agreement and disagreement.

3. Formulate options for solutions.

4. Evaluate options.

5. Act on options.

6. Formulate and act on final recommendations.

Preparation

Before each meeting, the chairperson and professional staff member meet to plan the session. They select the subjects that will enable the committee members to deepen their understanding of the issues and advance step by step toward the conclusions. They base their planning not only on their own judgment, but on what committee members have directed or indicated.

They try to anticipate the likely scenarios of what will happen. They ask: What views are the members likely to express on each concern? What positions are they likely to take? With what underlying reasons? What solutions may members advocate? What degree of support or opposition may there be for each option? By whom?

The chairperson and staff plan how to handle each possibility most effectively to guide the committee in moving toward its goals. Every eventuality cannot be foreseen. But many can, and the more prepared the chairperson and staff member are, the more successful the meeting is likely to be. That involves not only anticipating what may happen, but preventing diversions or obstructions.

The chairperson and staff member try to estimate how long the discussion of each subject is likely to be, and they allow ample time for it, with a tentative schedule to guide the chairperson in conducting the meeting. The schedule is not rigid, and the chairperson adjusts it to accommodate full substantive consideration, but it disciplines the chairperson to avoid needless repetition and prolonged discussion of trivia.

The official agenda is sent to committee members (usually with the minutes of the committee's previous meeting) prior to the meeting so that they can think about what will be considered and can come prepared to express their views. The agenda lists not only each subject, but also questions and issues within each topic that will be discussed.

In addition to the agenda, information is sent to provide committee members with the facts and analyses they need to understand the issues and consider the concerns knowledgeably. The materials are furnished at least ten days before the meeting, so that busy people with many other pressures will find the time to review them thoughtfully, but not so far in advance that members may forget some or much of what they have read. They also avoid sending voluminous packets that few if any members be able to read. Instead they succinctly provide the essence of what must be known and understood.

Leading organizations find that it is a fruitless waste to distribute the preparatory information at the meeting itself, where members can only scan the materials hastily, if they can read them at all. The only exception would be for developments or emergencies that may arise shortly before a meeting. In that event, time must be allowed for the members to read the documents as thoroughly as possible, and the chairperson and/or staff members explain or analyze them.

In preparing for the meeting, the chairperson and staff member also consult with the people who are to present reports at the session, to be certain that presentations will focus on the essence of the subject and will be well organized, succinct, and lucid.

Physical Setup

The organizations want their boards and committees to be a working group, with full, active interchange among the members. Since they understand that the physical arrangements for meetings may foster or inhibit such interchange, the organizations have the members sit around a table facing each other; they do not sit in rows and speak to each other's backs. Depending on the size of the group, the table may be oblong or round; a larger group may be seated around a square table with a hollow center or a U-shaped table. The table arrangement also enables committee members to take notes and refer to resource materials.

The meeting room should fit the group. It should be a comfortable room, large enough to accommodate the group, but not so large as to dwarf the meeting space.

The chairperson and professional staff member sit next to each other. They can thus consult with one another on situations that may arise during the meeting. The staff member can provide information the chairperson may need to deal with a question or issue; may call the chairperson's attention to people who have been asking to speak; or suggest to the chairperson other members who should be invited to comment on a subject during discussions because of their knowledge, judgment, and influence.

First Meeting

Organizations may have a brief reception at the first meeting of a newly appointed committee, so that members can get acquainted. The chairperson and staff member make a special point to welcome and chat with persons who have not been active previously in the organization, to convey how important their participation is. Name badges may be distributed for each member to wear. Name cards may be placed on the table in front of each member.

At the first meeting, the chairperson reviews the charge to the committee to make sure that all members understand what it is expected to achieve and the boundaries of its responsibility. After listing the issues to be addressed, chairpersons have often found it productive to invite the members to list the concerns they want considered. That exercise discloses what is most important to each person. It also emphasizes that the work of the committee will be shaped by the entire group, not by the chairperson and staff member alone. It underscores the organization's openness and desire to have the full input and guidance of all committee members.

In the same spirit, the agenda of each meeting allows a time period for members to initiate other elements for consideration beyond what the chairperson and staff member had scheduled.

Focused Discussions

The chairperson conducts a focused deliberation and the proceedings adhere to an agenda. The discussion is not permitted to wander into irrelevancies. The chairperson holds the committee discussion to one subject at a time, until the consideration of it has been completed. He or she does not permit the members to respond to extraneous comments that are unrelated to the subject being discussed. If the substance of such comments deserves consideration, the chairperson will postpone it until the committee has completed discussion of the matter being deliberated, and then have the committee address it.

The most important items are scheduled early on the agenda. Perceptive volunteers are well aware of the ploy in some organizations to clutter meetings with minor matters that take so much time that there is no opportunity to consider seriously the most important issues, which are introduced later. Volunteers thus may feel that their time has been wasted and complain that they are being "used." Leading organizations play no such games.

Reports

Reports that are for information only are generally mailed to the committee members, so that the meetings can concentrate on discussion. Oral reports at sessions are limited mainly to presentations that require discussion. They are succinct, well organized, and given by articulate people.

The reports are made primarily by volunteers, not by staff members. The volunteers' involvement attests to their knowledge, competence, and responsibility. It personifies and highlights the way the committee and the organization operate.

When the committee presents its progress reports, findings, and recommendations to the board, the same requirements consistently apply. Leading organizations do not tolerate reports that read like dull minutes—when committees met, who attended, what they talked about, in what sequence, item by item. Instead reports focus on what the board wants to know: what issues were confronted to carry

out the board's charge, what the findings were, what options were considered, what the committee recommends,
and why.

Participation

Chairpersons of successful committees skillfully stimulate
and draw out the participation of committee members in
consideration of the issues. They not only pose the issues
and questions listed in the agendas, they contact individual
members in advance of meetings to prompt them to speak
on subjects in which they have a strong interest or a depth
of knowledge and experience. In spreading the participation, they avoid domination by a few persons or by the staff
member.

Throughout the meetings, the chairperson and staff
member try to view each subject through the eyes of each
committee member. They take account of their values, priorities, and goals. They try to understand what is going on
in the members' minds as the discussion proceeds. They
are sensitive to how each one reacts to the views of others.
They can then relate to them with greater understanding,
obtain their participation more knowledgeably, and build
consensus more skillfully.

The chairperson and staff member encourage the expression of differences. They try to conduct a civilized, mature
debate on each issue. They attempt to demonstrate that
while people may disagree strongly and argue passionately,
they can do so without rancor.

They encourage the members to listen to each other without interruption, to maintain open minds, to weigh the merit
of what is being said, to learn from each other. They carry
on a process of reasoned analysis and evaluation.

The process adds spice, dynamism, and excitement to the meetings; builds pride in their quality and admiration of the participants; and results in gratification when a consensus is achieved.

The chairperson and staff member act as impartially as possible. But that does not keep them from voicing their judgments if and when they deem it necessary, after hearing the views of the members. The chairperson is usually a leader of the organization, respected for his or her broad experience, knowledge, wisdom, and commitment. The staff member has a uniquely broad and deep fund of information and expertise. The committee members look to these two people for insights and evaluations, when struggling with a knotty problem that is difficult to resolve and at other selected, appropriate times during discussions.

The chairperson and staff member avoid taking opposed positions during meetings, having resolved any differences in advance. And they consult with each other quickly before expressing themselves if new issues are raised during meetings and they suspect their judgments may differ.

If in the discussion at meetings unanticipated questions and issues are raised that have crucial implications and require information, analysis, and consultations beyond what is possible at the session, the chairperson and staff member can have the committee continue the consideration at the next meeting. The interval should be used to prepare the committee for the further discussion.

Follow-up of Meetings

After each meeting, the minutes are sent promptly—not weeks or months later—to all committee members. The minutes focus on the issues raised, the views expressed, and the actions taken.

The chairperson may telephone or write to members who presented reports or took other significant roles, to express appreciation and admiration for their contributions. Important members who were absent are telephoned by the chairperson or staff member to tell them that they were missed, to report on what happened, and to ask for their judgments and advice. The calls obtain the benefit of their reactions, underscore how greatly they are valued by the organization, and deepen their commitment to it.

The chairperson and staff member analyze the meeting to assess what gains were made, what problems and obstacles were encountered, and what opportunities were opened up. They list the follow-up actions that the committee directed or implied, how they will be carried out, who will be responsible for doing so, and with what time deadline. They review the agenda indicated for the next session and how to prepare for it.

Between committee meetings, the members are kept informed of how the actions they directed are being carried out, and of developments and events that affect the committee's responsibilities. They are provided with information to deepen their understanding of the issues they are addressing.

The activity between meetings verifies the meticulous implementation of what the committee directed, increases the group's ability to carry out its charge, sustains and heightens the members' interest and commitment, highlights the importance and dynamism of what they are doing, and underscores the seriousness of their responsibility.

11

---•:•●•:•---

UNDERSTANDING
THE ISSUES

The success of some nonprofits in resolving difficult, controversial issues, in contrast with the frustrations of other groups, is one of the most striking distinctions between the most productive organizations and the struggling ones. The next four chapters explain how leading nonprofits develop consensus out of differences, reach strongly supported decisions, and carry them out productively.

This process is unique to the nonprofit sector because of the unique character and requirements of the sector, in contrast with decision making by business and government, as explained in the section on decisions, in Chapter Thirteen.

People who do not understand the sector or have not participated in effective nonprofits may regard the process as cumbersome and prolonged. But those who have been involved in leading organizations know that the organizations reach decisions only as fast as the participants can, and that they do so soundly, with every effort to make each step an advancing one.

The ultimate test is the success in resolving difficult issues, with united commitment underlying them and a strengthened organization as a result. Such resolution could not have been achieved as well, or at all, without the process.

To deal with emergencies that require immediate decisions and actions, nonprofits have established crisis-management procedures that can be applied quickly and responsibly.

Foremost organizations make sure that their boards and committees consider major issues and policies on a solid foundation of facts. They do not assume that their decision makers uniformly have that knowledge. They provide it.

They have learned from their experience and from the failures of other organizations that when they begin to address a major concern, some decision makers may be uninformed, some only partly informed, and some misinformed. Even the best may not be fully informed.

Before the first meeting is held to address an issue, the organization's leaders and staff prepare the board and committee members. They inform the decision makers what the issue is, what it involves, why it is a concern of the organization, and why the leaders have brought it to the committee or board for analysis, judgment, and decision. They provide background and historic information that is pertinent and timely. They tailor it to what the members will grasp and understand. They try to have the members begin the discussion with as solid a basis of knowledge as possible.

How they provide the information is planned as carefully as what is provided. They do not burden people with massive materials that will not be read or raw information that has not been organized or placed within a context. They focus the data on what is germane to the organization and convey it concisely and lucidly, in a form that will invoke attention, hold it, and reward it.

This is not a one-time exercise. Additional information will be transmitted as the consideration progresses, as the depth of inquiry increases, as participants raise questions that require answers, as gaps in knowledge surface, and as the members themselves contribute their insights and experience.

In confronting the issues, leaders of successful organizations are sensitive to the lessons of history. A "must" is to check whether the organization has considered the matter in the past and, if so, what the outcome was; the pro and con arguments that led to the decision; the current relevance of those arguments; who held opposing views; and whether any of these persons are still members of the board.

They learn whether other organizations have considered the issue and, if they did, how they resolved it. If any have undertaken a service they are considering, they may consult with the other organizations' leaders and professionals. As the board and committee considerations proceed, they may arrange to have members visit other organizations to meet with their leaders and staff to obtain the benefits of their experience and insights directly, and to observe their operations at first hand. They may invite leaders and staff members of the organizations to meet with their committee or board.

More extensively, they may go to conferences that convene a wide range of organizations in their field of service, to gain further information, analyses, and judgments.

In the course of the consideration, they may call in academic and other experts to draw on their depth of research and knowledge. They may commission studies to obtain information not yet available. In doing so, they make sure that the studies focus on their concerns. When appropriate, progress reports are made to the committee and board to keep the decision makers informed of what is being discovered, to deepen their understanding, and to prepare them for the final findings and conclusions.

When appropriate too, some members of the committee or board are involved in the research, for their greater understanding and so that the findings will in part be their own findings. Such involvement also helps assure that the findings will be used by the committee and board, and not merely be put on a shelf to suffer the fate of too many unused studies.

The leaders recognize that issues are seldom one-dimensional. They can be dealt with productively only if the component elements are identified, understood, and addressed. The discussions center on the specifics and rule out fuzzy generalities.

While focusing on the specifics, members keep in mind their interrelationship and sequence. The leaders guiding the discussions are aware that some elements cannot be considered until others are first resolved.

> EXAMPLE:
> When the two organizations cited in the
> previous chapter undertook talks on their
> future relationship, they delayed discussion of
> merger until they had dealt with each of the
> responsibilities and functions they shared. In
> individual and successive discussions, they
> agreed that a dozen operations should be

unified, for better service and financial savings.
Combining those operations would bring them
very close to total merger. They then
considered corporate merger in the light of
those multiple functional consolidations, and
agreed on it.

The leaders understood that the wide initial differences
among the members would have prevented such agreement
if the option of full merger had been tackled at the beginning of the consideration. They had learned not to present,
entertain, or discuss ultimate total solutions initially, that
such an approach would entrap the group hopelessly
in generalities, and that the quagmire could block any
progress.

The leaders of effective organizations discipline themselves not only to concentrate initially on the concrete components of issues, but also to dig into the causes of problems
and to not limit themselves to symptoms. If they cut down
weeds while the roots are still in the ground, the weeds will
be back, with nothing accomplished. Such practices not
only fail to resolve issues; they undermine the credibility
and support of an organization and erode its services.

12

———————•◆•———————

UNDERSTANDING THE
DECISION MAKERS

E ssential as they are, facts alone do not determine decisions. People do. Understanding the decision makers is
as important as understanding the facts. In planning to have
the committee and board confront an issue or policy, the
leaders of the best organizations analyze how the members
are likely to approach and react to it. To the extent that
they know each of the members, they assess their motivations, priorities, and relationships, as well as other
influences that will determine their votes. Among the elements they appraise are the following:

Current Perceptions of the Issue

What perceptions of the issue do the members have? How accurate or inaccurate are they? What misperceptions must be overcome?

Values and Priorities

What values and priorities will the members apply in judging the issue? Who will regard it as crucial? Why? Who will regard it as peripheral? Why? Who will be indifferent?

Self-interest and Vested Interests

How will the members relate to the issue personally? Who will feel that they may gain from it? What might they gain? Who will fear they may lose something? What might they lose? Who will be on guard to make sure that nothing will be done to diminish a current service they prize, or to oppose an action that may affect another organization in which they are involved?

Personal Relationships

Who will lead in staking out positions, and who will almost automatically align with them because of respect for their knowledge and judgment, shared values, regard for their power and prestige, their business, professional, or personal relations, or their ethnic or religious affiliations; who will support their positions because of ambitions to advance in the leadership of the organization; who will not vote with them as a trade-off for reciprocated support on another issue?

In their planning, successful leaders look at the other side of the coin to forecast who may oppose a position because of the person who initiates it. Automatic opposition may be due to differences on a previous issue, general disagreement with the sponsor's underlying philosophy, personal rivalry, or other preconditions, so that little or no attention is paid to the merits of the proposal itself.

Reason or Emotion

Whose vote will be determined more by emotion than reason? For whom is this a passionate concern? For whom an intellectual one? Who feels so strongly about the issue that he or she will have little patience for calm deliberation? Who will be rigid? Who will be flexible?

Effective leaders analyze these and other motivations and influences as they plan realistically on how they may assure a thorough, reasoned consideration of the matter at hand.

Beyond sizing up the role each member may take, the leaders are alert to the sensitivities of the group as a whole. They have learned not to introduce an issue on the basis of how backward or derelict the organization has been in not confronting it and resolving it earlier, or in not having changed its policy, program, or procedures as the issue may imply. They know that such an approach might put the members on the defensive as a reflection of their shortcomings, and provoke them to justify themselves, concentrate on the critics, and bury the issue.

The approach therefore should be to the commitment of the members. It should be to undertake the consideration as part of a continuing search for achievement, by confronting vital issues that concern the organization; to probe whether the issue has the potential to increase the impact of its services; and to move the organization closer to its goals.

13

---•◦•◆•◦•---

Resolving Issues

Handling Differences

It has become increasingly necessary for a number of institutions to broaden the composition of their boards. Some have added representatives of minorities. Some have added leaders of the neighborhoods and clienteles they serve. Others have enlarged their boards or replaced veteran, aging members to include younger, outstandingly successful business and professional leaders, in order to obtain their involvement, acumen, and financial support.

New members often bring different backgrounds, interests, values, priorities, and goals to nonprofit organizations. The boards are no longer homogeneous bodies, composed of individuals long known to each other who agree on decisions graciously and quickly. Instead veterans have been confronted by strong-willed newcomers who vigorously press their own priorities. Often chairpersons and staff are neither trained nor experienced in handling the confrontations that can result. They have been dismayed and perplexed, groping to handle unforeseen disagreements. The result frequently has been division, conflict, bitterness, and disruption.

The leading organizations seek out diversity deliberately and with foresight, to strengthen and advance what they do. They understand that, in broadening their range and depth of ability, knowledge, and experience by taking in new members, they are virtually guaranteeing differences in judgments on major issues.

Effective organizations do not regard clashes of opinions as difficulties to be regretted or deplored. Rather they regard the differences as assets. They invite them, they expect them, and prepare for them. They believe, as Thomas Jefferson did, that "difference of opinion leads to inquiry, and inquiry leads to truth."

They understand that harmony in an organization is not achieved by suppression of views, that unity does not require uniformity, that diverse people can be united by a strong commitment to shared goals, by a mutual determination to find common ground, and joint actions to carry out their common purposes.

Because of this understanding, they can be open to hear the opposing views of their colleagues, to try to understand them, to consider them. The best leaders try to anticipate new ideas and opposing views. They do what Abraham Lincoln did: "When I am getting ready to reason with a man I spend one-third of my time thinking about myself and what I am going to say, and two-thirds thinking about him and what he is going to say."

Anticipating the differences, chairpersons and staff members try to plan and arrange for lucid expression of the differing judgments by their prime advocates, and for an orderly and thorough discussion. They seek a mature, civil debate, an experience that not only will achieve consensus and united action on the issue, but also will result in a more strongly bonded organization that is better able to handle future issues.

Important issues bring with them conviction and passion, and the debates that result can be exciting and stimulating. The discussions add spice to the organizations and strengthen the involvement and commitment of the members.

If the differences surface at the first meeting in which issues are addressed, the chairperson and staff member make clear to the group that these topics can be introduced and dealt with as part of the total agenda, but that they need not be discussed fully or resolved during the current meeting. They can be expressed, analyzed, and considered at subsequent meetings.

Thus members have the satisfaction of being able to voice their views and present them at the very beginning of consideration of an issue. At the same time, they are exposed quickly to the differing views of their colleagues. If the dissenters have talked primarily with people who shared their premises and conclusions, this may be the first time their views have been challenged face to face. It may be the first time they have heard alternative options authoritatively explained.

At the very least, this initial exposure is a learning and enlarging experience. It presses the advocates to reexamine their judgments and validate their positions; it demonstrates the necessity for convincing the others of the superiority of their positions.

The initial exposure to other viewpoints may solidify the convictions of opponents of an issue. But if they fail to convince others after being fully heard, they may feel compelled to seek compromise agreements that embody as much of their positions as they can obtain, to achieve as much as they can of what they seek. Or upon reflection, they may be persuaded that another option is better than theirs.

In conducting such discussions, the chairperson and staff member try to have the group concentrate on the substance of the issues. They clarify what the distinctions and differences are among the options, what they are based on, and how they might be resolved. They prevent irrelevancies from diverting the discussions—irrelevancies that may be inadvertently introduced by the comments of members, or that may be intentionally introduced and pressed to muddy the waters, distract the group from the substance, and prevent solutions.

One such trap is to focus the debate on the qualifications and personalities of the individuals who advocate an option, and not on the merits of what they propose, to center on who they are and not on what they say. The arguments may dwell on the alleged motives of people with an opposing view, their general philosophies, their other affiliations, positions they have taken in the past on other, unrelated issues, and other irrelevancies.

Effective chairpersons quickly rule out such detours. They skillfully move away from personality confrontations and bring the discussion back to the substance of the issue. They restore the consideration to a process of reasoning with one another, not attacking one another. They move the consideration away from a climate of winners and losers, for the shared objective of arriving at what will be best for the organization.

The ambience is that of colleagues who may initially differ greatly in their judgments, but who enjoy a debate that is intellectual and emotional, but always civil. They can argue passionately, but always with mutual respect. They can maintain their good humor and laugh together at the same jokes.

The chairperson's stance is that differences are not necessarily irreconcilable. His or her guidance is a constant effort to find whether options have common elements that can be fused into agreements.

When particularly complex components are introduced into the discussions, or where there are head-on opposing positions taken by factions of the group, it is often productive to have the leaders of the opposing elements meet with the chairperson and staff member between the full board or committee sessions to probe the differences in greater depth. In such intimate, concentrated talks it is often possible to work out agreements that can then be recommended to the full group. Such recommendations often provide the basis for agreement.

In seeking to move from differences and options to consensus, the chairperson and staff member define the specific elements that must be resolved in order to reach agreement on the issue. They schedule the elements most likely to be agreed upon first, and reserve the complex, difficult elements for last. As the discussion moves along, the chairperson and staff make a special point of identifying each point of agreement as it is achieved. Cumulatively the agreements form the growing base on which further concurrence can be built. These agreements underscore the progress and reinforce the motivation to move ahead to further agreement. Such an approach makes possible a final consensus that could not have been achieved if the issue had been tackled head on in its entirety at the start.

Example:

A community welfare planning council asked the leaders of two child-care agencies to meet jointly in order to explore the possible consolidation of their services. One organization provided foster home care, the other institutional residence. There was a long history of competition between the two, involving disagreements over which agency should serve children with various types of needs and problems. The joint committee, led by an impartial chairperson and staff member who had the trust of both agencies, included some mutually acceptable neutral members selected by the council so that the group would not comprise only antagonists.

The committee's initial meetings began to find common ground on the initial elements that were considered. At that point, the presidents of the two agencies took it upon themselves to meet alone, without the knowledge of the chairperson and staff member. The presidents concluded that the remaining elements could not be reconciled, and that the effort should be abandoned.

Instead of accepting the demise of the effort, the chairperson convened the committee and analyzed what had been achieved to date. He emphasized that the group had reached agreement on three of the five elements that had to be resolved. He defined the two questions that had not yet been considered and urged the committee to continue its efforts to work out agreement on them, as it had already succeeded on the other three. The committee concurred, pushed ahead with its discussions, resolved the remaining issues, agreed to merge, and carried out the merger.

In guiding discussions, effective chairpersons and staff members try to identify which elements the advocates hold most firmly, which they might compromise on, which they might concede on, and which they might trade off to opponents if the others would accept some of their positions. They seek solutions that all could "live with," in satisfaction if not delight.

The gates to final agreement sometimes may be opened by identifying individuals in each camp who have considerable influence with the others and who may be most ready to modify their stance. The chair and staff may consult with them between meetings. If common ground can be found, these influential people then undertake to persuade their colleagues to make the necessary concessions, modifications, or trade-offs.

The focus throughout is to have the group seek and attain what is most practical and most achievable in resolving the issue and advancing it closer to the goal.

Obstacles

Seasoned volunteer leaders and professional staff members open an issue for committee and board consideration aware of the catalogue of obstacles they may face. Among them are:

Apathy

Some members may have little or no interest in the subject. It is not a matter of concern to them, and they regard it as having little or no relevance to the organization. They see no point in spending time on it.

In preparing for the first meeting to address the issue, the leaders may talk with some of these members individually to try to convey the issue's importance to the organization, why other members urge that it must be addressed, and, if possible, how it relates to these members' own goals for the organization. These consultations are supported further by the preparatory materials supplied to all members before the first session, and thereafter by the substance and dynamism of the discussions.

Ignorance

Some members may know little about the issue. They may have little or no basis for discussing it, judging it, and deciding it. Effective leaders make sure that all members are prepared with a foundation of the essential facts before the consideration begins, as well as with additional facts as the discussions develop.

Cynicism

Some members may have no confidence that anything productive can be done about the issue. They may regard its consideration as a futile waste of time.

They often can be convinced, by being shown the experience of other organizations, that successful action on the issue is possible. They may be impressed by the determination and concerns of their colleagues, by individual consultations, or by other means that the matter is too important to be neglected. Or they may find themselves a small minority, bypassed by other members who are convinced that successful action on the issue is possible.

Fears

Some members fear change. They are content with what is. They fear the untested. Their fears may be based on emotion, not reason. They may regard any new proposal as a threat to the primary purpose and current services of the organization, which they cherish. They fear that the proposal may threaten the financial viability of the organization, the loyalty of its constituents, or the autonomy of the organization. If the experience of other organizations does not bear out their fears, they may still not be persuaded. Their retort may be, "We're different."

Good leaders try to learn the specific causes of such fears, and to overcome each of them by analysis and reasoning. They involve the fearful members in working out the decisions, building in safeguards that will reassure them. They may persuade such members that there is a minimum of risk by testing a new program or policy with limited pilot programs that can be evaluated before a major commitment or investment is made. They may project a phasing in of incremental efforts, and involve the doubters in the oversight, guidance, administration, monitoring, and evaluation of each step.

Threats to existing priorities and programs

If funding is required for proposed new services, some members may automatically object because "we haven't got enough money for what we are already trying to do." They regard it as a given that only after current services are fully financed can any new services be considered.

Members who feel this way have to be convinced either that more funds can be obtained for what is proposed (funds that could not be secured for what already is under way) or that if some funds were to be shifted from what the organization now does to proposed new initiatives, the organization would achieve more for the very purposes the objectors hold dearest. Such an approach may not succeed with all, and other efforts too may fail. Or the objectors may have to bow to a large majority of the board who differ with them.

Vested Interests

Volunteer leaders and professional staff deeply committed to a particular function or service may resist any modification of what they cherish. The activity has become a matter of principle for them, and it has been said that "hell hath no fury like a vested interest posing as a matter of principle."

Before opening an issue, effective leaders and staff members assess who may have such vested interests, and what safeguards may be required to protect what they treasure. If what they protect may indeed be affected, the leaders involve concerned members centrally and from the earliest stages in planning and carrying out the consideration of the issue. They are exposed fully to the views of others and to the total perspective and concerns of the organization of which their prized activity is a part. They participate in developing the decision. It becomes their decision, not the decision solely of others. If they remain rigid and find themselves in a small, outvoted minority, it is not because they have not been fully heard and involved.

Oversimplification

Some members may limit their concerns to superficial symptoms of a problem and ignore causes. They may assume single cause and effect relations, when in fact there are multiple causes and effects. Some press for shortcuts to complex problems, neglecting basic facts and analyses.

In their preparatory briefing of the committee or board, the successful chairperson and staff member point up the necessity of getting at the causes of a problem, and specify some of the complexities that are involved. As the delineations get under way, they resist "quick fix" solutions. During the discussions, the members build on that foundation with the questions they raise, the views they express, the concerns they reveal, and the opposing judgments they offer.

Overcomplication

At the other extreme are members who want to explore every possible nuance, who press for extensive extraneous research, or who urge the appointment of unnecessary sub-committees to examine various facets of an issue. Some of these pressures may be sincere searching, but some may be deliberate delaying tactics.

The chairperson, staff member, and others clarify what is required for in-depth analysis and judgment and what is overkill. Since many members value and budget their time and are eager to move ahead as quickly as they can, the overcomplication can usually be resisted and prevented.

False Premises

The chairperson, staff, and members have learned that some colleagues may reason from false premises and draw invalid judgments from them. They keep that in mind as they analyze the merit of what is argued. By identifying the quicksand underlying such arguments, they can refute the conclusions derived from them.

Personalities

The pitfall of basing objections on antagonism to the people who express the views, without regard to the substance and merit of what they advocate, has been noted earlier in this chapter. Such mind-sets are difficult to overcome since they are often based on emotion and on extraneous relationships, rather than on the issue.

The chairperson and staff member should try to learn the relationships of the members, to the extent that they can, before the issue is considered. Where possible, they avoid having the primary advocacy of positions and proposals voiced by individuals who will evoke opposition simply because of who they are. Such a precaution can be used when a position is shared by several people and there are options on who will take the lead in introducing and pressing it. But that may not always be the case. In that event, the chairpersons rule out discussion of personalities. They limit it to the substance of the issues.

Diversion to Another Subject

A classic tactic to obstruct progress is to digress to another subject, claiming that it is part of the issue and must be considered. Seasoned chairpersons and staff members have seen this ploy attempted and are alert to the possibility of its repetition. They distinguish for the group what is germane and what is not. They hold the discussion to the issue.

Analogies

Members may use irrelevant analogies to disparage and refute proposals. The irrelevancy is recognized by alert chairpersons and staff members, who point it out if other members do not see it.

Absence

Another tactic for delaying action is a request by a member to postpone discussion of a particular subject because of the absence of another member who is said to be especially concerned with it. The request may be genuine, or the absence may be deliberately timed to coincide with the day the subject is on the agenda.

The chairperson has to judge whether the delay would be harmless or is so related to other elements being discussed that it would impede the entire consideration; since there are some absences at almost all meetings, he or she also has to decide whether it is fair to those present to delay the discussion. The chairperson may thus rule on the request or may ask for the guidance of the group on the requested postponement.

"I want to think it over"

Instead of reacting to a proposed solution offered by other members, an influential leader whose position and vote is especially important may respond with, "I want to think it over." This may be a legitimate request for time to analyze and judge the proposal, or it may be a subterfuge to avoid dealing with it by starting a series of postponements.

The chairperson may grant the delay or may rule that the matter has been discussed thoroughly, with ample time for full consideration, and that consideration should proceed. If the delay is permitted, the chairperson sets a deadline date for the vote to prevent unwarranted delay.

"Let's wait until the next meeting to consider it"

A variation on the obstacle described above is a request to put off consideration of an important element of the issue until the next meeting. If this is a delaying tactic, it may be made with the assumption that there may be a somewhat different attendance at the next session so that the discussion may have to be repeated in part. When that happens, continuity and momentum are lost, and other delaying tactics can be introduced.

The chairperson and staff member have to weigh the merit of the request. If the matter was scheduled on the agenda in an advance notice to members, the discussion probably should not be postponed unless a valid reason is given, especially if it is part of a larger concern under consideration.

Members Leave Early

Some members may seek to delay consideration of an important element or issue by leaving the meeting early, and then request at the next session that the subject be reopened so they can participate in discussing it. Or they may ask beforehand that the matter be scheduled so late in the session that there is not time to discuss it fully.

The chairperson and staff member plan the sequence of the subjects to be considered, with estimates of the time each is likely to require, so that each may be discussed amply before the scheduled adjournment. If a matter has been fully considered with a quorum present, the topic probably should not be reopened unless there is an impressive, valid reason to do so and such a move is supported by the group as a whole.

Parliamentary Obstructions

Members may offer amendments, motions to reconsider, motions to table, and other parliamentary maneuvers to delay, divert, or prevent action.

The chairperson and staff must know parliamentary procedures and how to apply them, or make sure they have a member who is an expert parliamentarian available for guidance. A copy of *Robert's Rules of Order* is always at hand for reference.

Surprises

Surprises must always be expected in the consideration of major issues and policies. No matter how thoroughly leaders have planned and prepared the deliberations, no matter how fully they have consulted with and involved the full range of members, they cannot anticipate all that may happen. New objections may be raised by advocates with whom the issues had been discussed repeatedly and in depth; new concerns may be introduced; new subgroup alliances may be formed to press particular demands. Positions previously taken may be reversed. Agreements reached may be disavowed or broken. New interpretations may be made of what had been agreed.

Particularly disruptive are last minute "bombshells"—new objections at the very point of finalizing what had been agreed—that could destroy all the progress that has been made.

Seasoned leaders, especially the chairperson and staff member, are aware that such unforeseen complications can happen; they are prepared to react with poise to what leaders and staff with less experience and skill may regard as terribly upsetting disasters. At best, skilled leaders may be able to handle surprises by choosing quickly from the various options that can overcome the roadblock. At worst, they may be "puzzled but not upset," in the words of a veteran counselor.

They have several options. They may permit the issue to be reopened if they believe that what has been introduced merits it. They may treat the new development as part of the normal process of deliberations and handle it as they would any other element under consideration. They may ask the advocates to explain their new position, so that all may understand what is being sought and why. They may invite the comments of other members who are known to be able to refute what may be faulty proposals.

If he or she does not believe that the matter can be handled responsibly at the meeting or is uncertain about how to handle it, the chairperson may delay a response by ruling that the new elements are so important that the group should take time to consider them before the next meeting. In the meantime, the leaders can analyze more fully what has been introduced; can consult with others for their assessments and advice; can meet with the advocates to probe what is being sought; and can explore how the matter can be handled most constructively. They may ask other members who are especially influential with the advocates to try to work out acceptable solutions with them.

On the other hand, if they feel that there is no valid reason to turn back the clock and upset the entire progress of the discussions, they may ask the group at the meeting if the matter should be reopened. Before selecting that option, the chairperson and staff member should first assess and expect that the likely response will be to impressively reject reconsideration. If the group declines, the problem is resolved.

Agreement in Principle

Members may "agree in principle" on a proposed decision. Their vote to that effect may be a genuine underpinning of full agreement. But it may be an obstruction to give the impression that the matter has been basically resolved when it has not. Veterans know that an agreement in principle must be spelled out, and that in doing so they may face many differences on the specific elements that can block action.

> EXAMPLE:
> A hospital that had more land than its buildings occupied was pressed by the community to make some of the land available to a home for the aged that was about to build a new facility. The arrangement could save substantial costs and improve services, since a number of residents of the home were often treated at the hospital and several doctors served at both institutions.

Representatives of the two institutions met in a series of negotiations and arrived at an "agreement in principle" for the home to build on the hospital grounds. Both institutions felt they were acting under duress; neither actually wanted to share the land. The hospital preferred to hold the unused space for future expansion. The home for the aged feared that its autonomy and flexibility would be threatened by being located on hospital land. In further discussions, they could not find mutually acceptable provisions to carry out the "agreement." The home for the aged was built elsewhere.

Experienced chairpersons and staff have no illusions that "agreements in principle" mean an issue has been resolved. They learned the truth of Bismarck's statement that "when you say that you agree to a thing in principle, you mean that you have not the slightest intention of carrying it out in practice." They know that there is no actual agreement until all of the essential specifics have been defined and accepted.

Best Solutions

Some members may oppose agreements that are being reached because "they do not go far enough." They support what the agreements seek but believe that other members have compromised on only partial gains. They therefore vote against the "better" because they insist on the "best."

In such cases, the majority usually are convinced that agreement on the "best" is not yet attainable and that to insist on it would block any progress. They reason that no decisions are perfect or final and that advances are often incremental. The most that they can agree on at the present time can be extended in the future, when the organization will have the benefit of additional, tested experience. In fact, even the "best" might be subject to change in the light of new circumstances and growing knowledge and opportunities.

Organization leaders should make a point of interpreting negative votes because the actions did not go far enough not as opposition to the decision, but as pressure to do more of what the decision mandates.

Editing Reports

Obstacles can be set up even after a committee or board has resolved an issue or policy and voted a decision. One such barrier is the pressure to "edit" or "summarize" the final report that sets forth the conclusion and the reasons underlying it. A claim may be forwarded that the committee's report is too long and detailed for all of the board members to read and digest, or that the board's report is too lengthy to be absorbed by the constituents.

Those who urge such editing want to be on the committee that will draft the summary. They press to omit important elements as "details," and to oversimplify and obscure the meaning of other provisions.

Experienced leaders are on guard against this tactic. They include an authentic executive summary in the report, and draft it to convey accurately the essence of the full report. They resist the pressures for ex post facto "editing committees."

Decisions

As organization leaders open a major issue or policy for consideration, their goal is to reach a consensus decision. They know what consensus is and what it is not. They seek consensus on the largest attainable area of agreement—the highest common denominator, not the lowest.

What they need not seek is unanimity. A small minority does not block the will of a large majority. As John Gardner has observed: "Everyone does not have to agree for the consensus to be effective. It is only necessary that there be rough agreement among a substantial proportion of those men and women whose intelligence, vigor, awareness and sense of responsibility mark them as shapers of community purpose. For anyone interested in innovation, the consensus is equally important. If a society enjoys a reasonable measure of consensus, it can indulge in a very extensive innovation without losing its coherence and distinctive style. Without the durability supplied by American consensus, our fondness for innovation and diversity would commit us to chaos and disorder."

Consensus is often the quickest action, not the slowest. Shortcuts without full consideration, full understanding, involvement, and commitment are frequently stillborn failures. The vote on an issue is not the final determinant. It is the actions that flow from the vote that are crucial. Consensus votes give the strongest assurance that effective implementing action will carry out the vote.

Voluntary organizations are different from business and government in that they cannot compel their members to carry out a vote. A 51 to 49 majority may legally authorize an organization to act, but with 49 percent opposed, the support may be too weak to carry out the vote effectively. A minority retains the right to continue its opposition and to agitate against the majority position. A large, powerful minority can vitiate a slim majority vote.

The aim is to avoid having "winners" or "losers" in a decision; to have people work together within the organization, not against each other; to reach conclusions that will achieve the most for the organization's mission and services, to which all are committed; to build a sense of "ownership" of the decisions, by having full participation of all members in arriving at the decision.

Majorities do not ignore minorities in nonprofit organizations. They try to accommodate them, if possible. They involve them in implementing the decisions. If some opponents stay on the sidelines while the decisions are being carried out, they are not ostracized. Their convictions and integrity are respected. They have an open invitation to participate whenever they may be ready. If the implementation proceeds and succeeds, the opponents often do not want to remain isolated. They want to be part of the success.

The goal of consensus is to build unity of action out of an initial diversity of opinion.

Options

The leaders of effective organizations do not open consideration of major issues and policies with minds that are blank slates. They begin with tentative judgments on what outcomes might be most desirable. In forming their assessments, they have taken into account the views that were revealed in their preparatory consultations with the most influential members of the board. They know what differences to expect in the discussion, and that other views will surface as the consideration proceeds.

The leaders initially do not present their own preliminary solutions. They listen to the members, learn from them, and search for common elements with which to build consensus. They adjust their views to incorporate what they have gained from the discussions.

They know, too, that there may not be only one best solution. As two or more options may appear to have equal merit, the advantages and disadvantages of each are identified and evaluated. Beyond their own assessments, the volunteer leaders expect the staff to analyze the options in depth, based on all of the information and experience they can obtain, to report whether any of the options have been tested by others, whether the testing was done under comparable conditions, what advances were achieved, and what flaws were revealed.

The leaders and staff members take into account the current competence of the organization, its strengths, its experience and expertise, its human and financial resources, its potential and its limitations. They are eager to embark on as much as can be achieved, but are alert to what is realistically possible.

They analyze the financing that will be necessary for each option. They have seen programs that have been launched with strong ideological support, but that fail because decision makers did not provide the funds required to carry them out adequately. They take into account the interests of the organization's major sources of support and may involve some of their major contributors in making the decisions, in order to build their commitment into the outcome.

Each option is weighed for its own merit, and for the effect the decision may have on all of the organization's services. Will it enhance or weaken other operations? Will it increase or erode the organization's total effectiveness? Will it build greater commitment and support? Will it unify or fragment the members?

If the leaders and staff members find that consensus can be reached only on a willingness to have a pilot test of a solution rather than a continuing commitment, they assure that the pilot will provide a reliable evaluation. They specify that it will operate long enough to genuinely test it, that it will be adequately financed and staffed, that it will have the necessary volunteer oversight, and that the tools for monitoring and evaluation are built in from the beginning.

Another option successful organizations adopt in venturing into untried waters is to authorize, in advance, contingency modifications for correcting inadequacies that may be revealed and for adapting to changing conditions and opportunities.

Agreement May Not Always Be Possible

Leaders understand that it may not be possible to reach consensus on every issue. The differences of judgment may be too great to be overcome. It may be wiser to postpone a vote rather than to resolve an issue by a majority that is too slim to carry out the decision effectively. If it appears that a proposal with merit will be rejected now but might be approved after a time interval, they avoid a negative vote rather than have to reverse the defeat later. Delay can make possible more education, preparation, discussion, consultations, and negotiations. It can allow for a cooling of emotions, enable opponents to collaborate on other matters, and provide time for a building of greater mutual respect and trust.

Momentum

The chief volunteer and professional officers and other leaders of effective organizations keep in mind all of the above possible outcomes in approaching the consideration of issues and policies. They guide the discussion, with a sense of timing, through the simplest to the more complex elements. They do not hurry the process. They avoid oversimplification and superficiality. But they do not permit the deliberations to bog down in fruitless repetition, or in peripheral and inconsequential details.

They maintain momentum, crystallizing and articulating specific agreements as they are reached, documenting the progress being achieved, and building a base for further consensus. They nurture a growing sense of the importance of what is under way. They share with others their gratification with the challenge, the progress being made, and the thoroughness and integrity of the process.

No matter how difficult the obstacles and complexities, the leaders are persistent. They are determined to outlast anyone who may seek to prevent action by delay, diversions or obstructions.

Compromise

In seeking a decision or resolution, the leaders understand that compromise may be necessary. They perceive how compromises are obtained. They have learned from business and politics, as well as from their experience with nonprofits, that people often start by demanding more than they expect to get, negotiate with opponents to win as much as possible, and then "compromise" to achieve all they actually wanted.

In working to build consensus, the leaders try to identify within the opposing arguments the core positions and the "give aways." They distinguish between the principles that cannot be compromised and the flexible, specific measures that can be adjusted to satisfy the principles.

Progress Reports

Committees that are considering issues keep their governing boards informed of their progress through periodic reports on their work. These reports build the board members' understanding of the elements being addressed, the options being considered and the pros and cons of each, and the agreements that are being reached.

Some reports are mailed to the members. Others are presented orally at board meetings, to obtain the benefits of the board members' questions, reactions, comments, and advice as guidance for the committees' further work. The reports maintain the interest and involvement of the governing body. They prepare the board for final consideration of and action on the committees' recommendations.

The reports are carefully crafted. They focus explicitly on the issues and major elements being considered, the options and the pros and cons of each, the conclusions reached to date, and the concerns yet to be resolved.

The writers understand that the reports must be accurate and lucid, must attract and hold attention, and must be readily understood. They are sensitive to diversity among the board members as readers or listeners. The writers ask themselves: Will the reports be understood as the writers intended? Will the wording facilitate or obstruct progress? Will it arouse or remove fears? Will it be regarded by opposing advocates as one-sided? Does the content and language objectively convey what is important to proponents and opponents?

In order to prevent premature misuse of progress reports, the working interim documents are prominently labeled "confidential—not for circulation or publication." Readership is limited to the board members. If the reports get into the hands of people who lack the board members' background, knowledge, and responsibility, they may be misunderstood as stating final conclusions rather than matters under consideration. Such misconceptions can lead to serious problems.

This does not mean that the reports are completely confidential. Committee and board members inevitably discuss the content with others, but such discussion generally involves explanation and interpretation and thus is different from a perusal of a document without preparation and without a full understanding of the background or basis of what is under way, or of the context in which the committee is working.

Oral reports to the boards of leading organizations are succinct and articulate, conveying the depth and dynamism of the process. They highlight the questions on which the board's comments and guidance are desired. They exist in contrast with monotonous reports that sound like sequential minutes of meetings, which often are disjointed and unfocused.

Final Recommendations

The final findings and recommendations of committees are transmitted to the board prior the meeting at which the board will consider and act on them, so that the members may study the report, reflect on it, and be prepared to discuss it. The chairperson and staff member do not take for granted, however, that all board members will have done their homework. At the meeting, they have the committee chairperson summarize the report's essence and highlight what the board needs to consider and decide.

In planning the discussion, the committee chairperson will have arranged for members of the committee to speak after the summary of the report is read, amplifying the reasons for their support of the recommendations and buttressing them with their endorsements. They avoid having an unbroken succession of opponents speak first while the supporters sit back passively and silently. The opponents are given full opportunity to voice their views, early and fairly.

But the chairperson avoids an initial monopoly of discussion by the opposition, which would tend to distort the committee's stance and set up a negative framework for the board's consideration.

The board's decisions are worded precisely, to prevent or minimize unwanted interpretations. The precision is meticulous, in order to provide a full, uniform understanding and to assure the members that planned implementation is clearly defined and will be completely faithful to what the board authorized. The language approved by the board is not altered thereafter, except by the board. The text is not "refined" or "edited" by officers or staff, unless the board authorizes it.

Emergency Decisions—Crisis Management

Emergencies may require immediate decisions without committee process or even a meeting of the full board, especially if the board members are scattered across a wide geographic area. Leading organizations have prepared in advance to take such actions. They have well-defined procedures in place, authorized by the board. They do not have to hastily or frantically find ad hoc improvisations for each emergency.

The procedures are adapted to the types of organizations, and to the size and location of their governing bodies. Among the provisions are the following:

- An immediate meeting of the board, if possible.
- A telephone conference of the board, if practical—usually if there are more than twenty-five board members.

- A meeting or telephone conference of the smaller executive committee.

- A meeting or telephone conference of the officers.

- Delegation of authority to a designated group, including the chief volunteer officer, the chief professional officer, and others.

The board sets limits on the authority of individuals who are designated to act. If expenditures are involved, a ceiling is placed on the funds that can be committed. All actions must adhere to the organization's policies. The board is informed immediately of the decisions taken, with full explanation, and the actions are reviewed by the board at its next meeting.

14

IMPLEMENTATION

Votes to resolve an issue are meaningless unless they are carried out, and carried out well. The boards of leading organizations understand that. They spell out the required implementation in their decisions.

They stipulate who will be responsible for the implementation; set goals and timetables for achievement; specify the additional staffing that may be required, the financing and how it will be provided, the monitoring and evaluation that must be built in, and the continuing lay oversight to assure that the board's intent is fulfilled. They require continuing accountability, with regular reports on the progress of the implementation.

The quality of implementation is paramount. Poor performance can be disastrous, destroying the effort and vitiating the decision. It can invalidate a sound decision and an essential program by confusing onlookers about the cause of the failure; the plan and the decision may be discredited rather than the botched implementation, and this can block a revival of the effort for years to come.

The harm done by flawed implementation extends beyond the failure of a particular program. It impairs the credibility of the organization, undermining its stature and support.

In order to prevent such failure, leading organizations plan and organize implementation of their decisions meticulously. They realistically assess how readily progress can be made. They do not build up false expectations. They know that many programs must be developed over a period of years, that some things cannot be attempted until others are done first. They set multi-year goals and schedules. They phase in the staffing and financing, specifying what will be added each year.

The organizations set attainable first objectives, to demonstrate achievement as soon as possible. They instill confidence by productive actions that bring results. They demonstrate their ability to carry out what they promise. They build commitment to further development and additional financing.

They stipulate the elements of the implementation, attend to detail, and shun fuzzy generalities. They delineate the successive steps, to the extent possible, and make sure that all are carried out.

They coordinate all aspects, so that each is consistent with and reinforces the others, and so that cumulatively they advance the achievements.

At the same time, the organizations maintain a flexibility that allows them to adjust the implementation to the realities they encounter. They adapt to changing conditions, information, and resources. They learn from experience what does not work as expected, and what proves to be more productive than they anticipated. They revise and replace the former and reinforce the latter.

The quality and competence of the people who conduct the implementation are critical. They can often be the most important cause of success or failure. Over and over again sound decisions, plans, and programs have failed because of the inadequacies of the volunteer leaders and staff members who oversaw and administered them. The professionals' knowledge and skills, especially, must meet the requirements of the new endeavor.

Grievous mistakes have been made when staff members who were outstanding in what they had been doing previously were employed for new responsibilities that required different skills. They have sometimes floundered, stymied the effort, and even have had to resign. The organizations have had to recoup, employing new staff with the requisite qualifications, overcoming delays, restoring confidence, and starting anew.

EXAMPLE:
An organization appointed a very prestigious expert committee to analyze the needs of a field of its responsibility that it had neglected and that was reported to be in dire straits. It selected a chairman with a depth of knowledge in that field, a highly articulate and personable man who was respected by the eminent members of the committee. He chaired the committee skillfully, and it brought back an impressive set of findings and recommendations that won the highest praise

of the organization and an enthusiastic
commitment to carry out the recommendations.

The organization thought it would be a tremendous coup
if it could employ the chairman to direct the new program,
and congratulated itself on being able to obtain him.

But the implementation required different qualities and
skills than the chairmanship of the committee. The former
chairman soon found himself at odds with the volunteer
leaders responsible for oversight, and with the professional
colleagues whose cooperation and involvement were required. These people, who understood what he did not, tried
earnestly to help him, but without success. After a few years
he resigned, but the initial enthusiasm and commitment
had been lost, and it took additional years for the effort to
get back on track.

There is no guarantee that an individual selected to direct
an entirely new and untried effort will be the right choice.
But the leading organizations have learned that when they
have made a mistake in appointment, they must not try
to "live with it." That delay could be fatal to the effort, as
well as inhumane to the person, who struggles with frustration and personal unhappiness. The organizations make a
change as soon as feasible, and as sensitively and consider-
ately as possible.

The full involvement of volunteer leaders for the oversight of implementation is essential. The organizations
select for oversight people who were involved in developing
and making the board's decision to undertake the action.
These leaders understand the action and are committed to
it. They represent the board to assure that decisions are
carried out faithfully, authentically, and effectively.

The staff alone cannot supply what the volunteer leaders
provide. They provide knowledge, experience, resources,

and skills that are of enormous value in carrying out the decisions.

The best organizations tap for oversight responsibility some of the opponents of the decision and some individuals who were lukewarm. Such persons are not a majority of the oversight group, but they are not excluded. Once they become a part of the implementation, they are not then on the sidelines, ready to criticize every real or imaginary shortcoming of the action. They know what is happening from the inside; their understanding is deepened. They also can influence the implementation. Their doubts are taken into account in shaping the implementation; attempts are made to avoid the feared negatives and reassure the doubters. They share the credit of the successes and thus their commitment to the organization is enhanced.

Implementation is a new opportunity to involve volunteers who have not been active in the organization. Their participation can enrich the effort and the organization.

If additional funds will be required, the board has defined the amount, the potential sources, and how the funds will be obtained, and has committed itself to assure them. This is spelled out as part of the board's decision, before the implementation begins.

Boards are realistic about the amount of funds that will be sought, and what can be expected. The projections are not vague hopes. The boards know that unless the required financing is obtained, the action should not be undertaken.

The boards hold the oversight committees and staff accountable for the implementation. They instruct the volunteers and staff members to monitor the implementation continuously, to evaluate it internally (and externally, when appropriate). They direct the volunteers and staff members to report to the board periodically on the progress being made, the obstacles encountered, the achievements and the shortcomings, and the adjustments that will be required.

15

MONITORING,
EVALUATING,
REPORTING

Monitoring

Successful organizations monitor their services and operations continuously. They regard monitoring as essential to assure that they carry out effectively what they intend. It enables them to reinforce what is succeeding, to revise what is falling short, to prevent partial failures from becoming total failures, and to change shortcomings into successes, if possible.

The organizations monitor to make sure that their implementation carries out their commitments and projections, that they adhere to their timetables, that they are progressing toward their goals. If they encounter unexpected obstacles and delays, if they find it necessary to adjust and change, the monitoring identifies where corrections should be made. It helps define next steps and priorities that should be in place.

All participants in management, administration, and operations are involved. The staff members performing the services continuously assess their experience. They share their analyses with their supervisors. The supervisors and administrators keep the oversight committees informed. The oversight committees keep the boards informed.

The organizations monitor financing as well as services. They assess whether funds are adequate. If they are insufficient, the organizations can promptly decide whether to seek more funds, reallocate the use of their funds, or reduce costs to match income and prevent deficits and debts. If organizations find that costs are not as great as expected, they can reduce the financing accordingly.

Authentic monitoring can be done only if organizations build in tools at the beginning of services to provide the facts required for analyses and judgments.

In any new programs, actual experience is almost certain to bring to the surface elements that could not be anticipated. Conditions may change between the time that plans are made and programs begin. If programs are falling short of what was sought, organizations must learn and determine why they are not working out as intended. Were the goals unrealistic? Were the designs faulty? Were the projected programs inadequate to deal with the complexities of the problems and needs? Were the plans sound but the implementation faulty? Did the staff fully understand what had to be done? Was the staff qualified to carry it out? Were the auspices a handicap? Exposing and confronting the negatives frankly is indispensable to prevent failures.

Recognition and admission of shortcomings do not taint an organization. On the contrary, they add to a group's credibility. People know that nothing new and untried is certain or likely to be perfect. They don't believe or trust organizations that never admit inadequacies.

Evaluations

Beyond the ongoing monitoring, effective organizations make periodic evaluations to appraise the aggregate of what they do. They evaluate particular programs, services, innovations, units, and departments, or even their entire operations. They reexamine their missions, goals, responsibilities, policies, priorities, and services; their administration and financing; and their volunteer and professional human resources.

They fundamentally assess the results of what they do and the impact they make. Are they progressing toward their goals? Are they achieving them? Are they making changes in the needs and problems they address? Are the needs being alleviated or overcome?

Evaluations are made both internally and externally. Internal evaluations are made by the volunteers and staffs of the organizations. They are necessary in order to determine whether to continue or modify the organization's services.

External evaluations are conducted by experts who are not part of the organizations. They are enlisted in order to assure that the judgments are objective and detached, to obtain the expertise of people who have broader knowledge and experience than the staff, and to give credibility to the findings and the recommendations that emerge.

External evaluations are undertaken selectively. They may be designed to assess the experience with new programs or for particular functions. Some organizations periodically review and evaluate their entire operations.

As in monitoring, the tools to make evaluations possible are built into the designs of new services and operations, so that essential facts will be available for analysis and evaluation.

The engagement of external evaluators is not an automatic application of a uniform blueprint. Each evaluation is custom-made, tailored to the requirements of the organization and what is being assessed. The scope, depth, and character of the evaluation is shaped to fit the subject of the appraisal. The costs of the examination are specified and assured before the evaluations are undertaken.

The evaluations try to link results with causes. They seek to correct deficient services that have not been productive because they have mistaken or ignored the roots of the problems, because the remedial actions were inadequate to achieve solutions or inappropriate for the problems, or because the operations were incompetently carried out.

Where the evaluations verify progress and achievements, they point the way to further support for what is succeeding.

In human needs and services, it is often difficult to link cause and effect. Many factors impinge on conditions and problems. The evaluations must identify multiple causes and their relative impact. They must avoid the oversimplifications, myths, and superficialities that often befog the consideration of such services.

Evaluations of human services may be more complex and difficult than in business. While some services can be measured quantitatively, others cannot. Qualitative assessments pose special obstacles to objectivity and precision.

Such complexities do not deter leading organizations from making evaluations. Rather these groups make sure, to the best of their ability, that the evaluations are as penetrating, accurate, and authentic as possible.

They put a premium on precision. They avoid generalizations, such as labeling operations as "successful" without explanations of what "success" is. Instead they specify what changes were achieved, what gains took place, and what was accomplished.

Evaluations are not confined to examining what has taken place. They are forward-looking, to point the way to more productive services. They help shape what the organizations' goals should be, and what policies and priorities should be in place.

Productive evaluations do not limit themselves to what the organizations have been doing. They are alert to what has not been undertaken or done, and to gaps in the work that should be addressed to carry out the responsibilities of the organization. They inform the organizations of emerging new needs, of innovative services that other similar organizations have created and that should be examined for possible emulation or adaptation. They open up greater possibilities for achievement.

Whether internal or external, evaluations are not made solely by staff members and outside experts. The participation of volunteer leaders is essential and fundamental. Evaluations assess the basic purposes, services, and administration of organizations. They affect future goals, policies, and priorities. The development of the recommendations requires the full understanding, formulation, and commitment of the volunteer leaders who govern the organizations.

Volunteer leaders and staff members share fully in internal evaluations, in the analyses, in weighing what is learned, and in determining what should be done.

In external evaluations, the experts engage the volunteer leaders as well as the staff in examination and analyses. The experts need the volunteer leaders' involvement to understand the motivations and control of what they are investigating, the realities of the operations, and the causes of what they find.

Successful evaluations are carried out under the oversight of committees that include the most influential volunteer leaders of an organization, reflecting a cross section of constituencies. The committees define the scope of the evaluations mandated by the boards, and outline the character of the examination they seek. They engage the experts for the external evaluations.

Oversight committee members are thoroughly engaged in analyzing the findings as they emerge, formulating the recommendations, bringing the findings and recommendations to the board, supporting and advocating them in the board's consideration, gaining the board's approval, and assuring thereafter that the board's decisions will be carried out most effectively.

Sandra Gray of the Independent Sector has summed it up: "Evaluation is part of a continuous process of learning and renewal. It enables organizations to direct change rather than be directed by it, to take a proactive stance rather than a reactive one." It "demonstrates that they are open, accountable, and mission-driven . . . helping organizations use evaluation for effectiveness, empowerment, and excellence."

Reporting

Once a decision has been made to undertake new or revised policies, services, and programs, effective organizations do not allow them to become routine or to be taken for granted. The excitement that sparked the decision of the leaders and staff members to devote energy and funds to implement services and programs is nurtured to keep what is being done exciting and inspiring.

The leaders and staff are kept informed of the actions taken, the urgency of the needs, the lessons that are learned, the impact of the actions, the problems that are encountered, and the modifications that are made to overcome them. They confirm that the financing requirements are being carried out.

The best organizations have found it essential to maintain confidence in what was initiated, to demonstrate that they are delivering on their promises and commitments. Their oversight committees and staff members report regularly to the boards, to keep their interest alive, to deepen their understanding and their commitment, and to underscore the meticulous implementation of the boards' directives. The reports often include a scorecard for the board, listing specifically the recommendations that were to be carried out, the target dates for each, which targets have been fulfilled, and what remains to be done.

The reports attest to the integrity of the implementation, and build respect for the actions and for the organization. They increase the readiness of the boards to address other issues, needs, and innovations in the future.

Reports on implementation are made not only to the board, but to the major donors who finance the implementation. They confirm to the donors that the commitments made in soliciting their contributions are being carried out, inform them of the gains being achieved as a result of their generosity, and express the continued gratitude of the organization.

Accountability and reporting are not left to chance, nor are they spontaneously improvised. They are required as part of the board's decision to authorize an innovation and are specified in the directive for its implementation.

16

——◆——

COMMUNICATION

Ongoing communication is a "must" for leading organizations. It is essential among volunteers, between volunteers and professional staff, within the staff, with constituents, and with the general public.

Communication builds understanding of what the organization's services and achievements are; it strengthens commitment and involvement. It keeps an organization in the forefront in the minds of its volunteers, in competition with many other pressures and distractions.

Successful communication is carefully planned, with a strategy. It spells out the markets to be addressed, and the priorities among them—the officers, the board, committee members, major contributors, other contributors, constituents, and others. It defines the purposes and goals of what is to be transmitted. It is coherent and relates the message to the market.

The communications program is budgeted, detailing how much will be spent and on what, within policies set by the board. The program specifies the budget, how it will be financed, how it will be staffed and with what oversight, and how it will be monitored and evaluated.

The most successful organizations understand that their communication must be expertly done and must be of the highest quality. They understand that they are competing with the best in commercial and other nonprofit communication for the attention of their audience. Many organizations employ creative, expert communications staff. Many obtain the invaluable guidance and skills of volunteers who are outstanding leaders in communications, public relations, and advertising to help plan and create the communication, often to help produce it, and to give continuing oversight to it.

The most effective communication is pithy and as brief as possible, in order to gain and hold the attention of recipients rather than be put aside for "later," which often means never. It concentrates on the essence of what is to be transmitted and is related to the concerns of the people receiving it. It is lucid and avoids murky jargon. If documents must be lengthy, they include brief summaries.

The communication is timely. New developments are reported promptly, before they become stale.

The organizations are alert to new technical developments that are emerging to facilitate communication. They apply what is appropriate to them and to their message. Today, printed matter often can be produced more attractively, flexibly, and inexpensively than in the past. The organizations utilize the telephone not only for individual contacts, but for conference-call discussions with small groups.

National and regional organizations employ closed-circuit television for carefully selected agendas. They take advantage of the immediate communication made possible by fax and electronic mail. They use videotaping for visual messages. They individualize and personalize communication whenever appropriate and feasible, especially in letters of thanks for services and major contributions.

The communication keeps the recipients informed of what the organization is doing, and with what impact. If successes are achieved, it is vital that they be known. People are attracted to organizations that succeed.

If organizations are encountering obstacles and difficulties, that too is reported to appropriate persons, together with what the organizations are doing to overcome the problems. The recipients are informed of emerging issues that must be considered, and of developments affecting the missions, activities, and finances of the organizations.

Communication gives volunteers, staff members, constituents, and others a greater understanding of the total scope of the organization. Annual reports on an organization's services and finances are substantive, attractive, and lucid. They recount the organization's mission, purpose, and priorities, review explicitly what has been done to carry them out and what was achieved, along with any shortcomings. They stipulate the sources and amount of financial income, and explain expenditures. They analyze the implications of the year's experience for the year and years ahead, and project the priorities that will be pursued.

A number of organizations send their board members monthly newsletters on pertinent developments. Many report to their major contributors and constituents periodically.

Communication is two-way, not only from the organization but to the organization. It encourages board and committee members, major contributors, and constituents to communicate their comments, questions, judgments, and advice on their own initiative, not only in response to what the organizations request.

In soliciting such views, organizations know that many people will not respond. Yet they are not discouraged from continuing to invite comments. At the very least, they have informed the recipients, have kept them involved, and have manifested their continuing importance by seeking their advice.

The best organizations knowingly open themselves to criticism as well as commendation. They prefer to have the critics bring their views directly to them, rather than go public with their complaints. They examine the merits of these dissents. They respond to them, providing pertinent facts when necessary and, when appropriate, informing them of differing views that must be taken into account. They selectively discuss the differences with some of them. They make clear that the criticisms are respected and fully considered. And, when merited, the organizations make changes that are urged.

Organization volunteer leaders and staff members personalize communication as fully as possible. They telephone selected influential individuals to inform them on key matters and to discuss important developments. They meet with such individuals for face-to-face communication and consideration. Whenever possible, personalized communication is linked to active involvement in the governance and services of an organization. Nothing builds greater understanding and commitment than involvement, which is the ultimate form of communication. An organization is then "we," not "them."

Communication is not confined to board members, contributors, and constituents. The leading organizations are aware that they are part of their communities, of their region, of the nation. They address such larger audiences to communicate the needs and problems they are confronting, and the actions they are taking to overcome them. They skillfully utilize newspapers, magazines and journals, radio, television, and other media.

They selectively address already assembled audiences convened under various auspices, though they do this with safeguards, sending articulate speakers who are fully knowledgeable about their organizations and who have been chosen to relate especially to the particular audience. The organizations make sure in advance that their role in a meeting will be a respected one; that they will not be squeezed in reluctantly, as a favor, "for a few minutes"; that their representatives will be appropriately introduced; and that their involvement will be deemed important.

Internal communication within the staff is essential. All staff members, including support staff, are kept informed of the organization's total activities. The best internal communication relates what each person does to what all the others do, giving each a greater understanding of the larger goals that his or her work helps to achieve.

Executives communicate continuously with their staffs, and encourage their staff members to communicate with them and with each other. The communication is carried out systematically, both individually and in frequent, scheduled staff meetings, to inform, discuss, and share judgments. Newsletters are circulated to report what other staff members are doing. Communications help weld all into a working team that shares responsibilities and supports all members in advancing the total achievement of the organization.

17

———◆———

INDIVIDUAL
CONSULTATIONS

Individual consultations and relationships are vital in the strengthening and decision making of nonprofit organizations. Their role and significance have been underscored throughout this book.

Volunteer leaders and professional staff members of leading organizations understand the importance of consultations. They plan for them, develop them, and utilize them thoroughly.

Individual consultations largely determine who will lead and govern the organizations. They enable organizations to identify, attract, and involve the ablest, most influential, and most productive volunteers to carry out their missions.

Effective CVOs continuously consult with their fellow officers, with their most influential board members, with committee chairpersons, and with staff members. Chairpersons consult with their key members and with the staff. Volunteers consult with other volunteers. Volunteers and staff consult in a close, productive partnership.

The CVO and the CPO especially share information, exchange ideas and proposals, develop plans, resolve differences, prepare for board and other meetings, assess the outcome of the sessions, and plan the follow-up and much more. The same is true of committee chairpersons and staff members.

A professional conducting an executive search may consult with each member of the search committee to make sure that all have a common understanding of the criteria and priorities established by the committee, so that they evaluate the candidate with the same measures.

In fund raising, individual consultations enable the organizations to discover the foremost new prospects to be approached for major annual gifts; to select priority prospects for planned giving to endowment funds; and to establish philanthropic funds and supporting foundations in the organization. Consultations help in the designation of individuals who have the best personal relationships for soliciting prospects and obtaining maximum gifts.

Individual consultations make possible many of the advances in organizations. CVOs and CPOs especially consult with the most influential donors and board and committee members to explore their awareness, knowledge, and views on the organization's needs and challenges, to learn whether they would favor or oppose proposals for change, to get their overall appraisal of how the agency is performing, and to gain their support for what is required.

The organization's planning depends substantially on individual consultations to assure an essential understanding of what will be addressed and the need for planning, and to define the planning. Continuing consultations characterize the process as planners assess findings, analyze their implications, and shape resulting recommendations.

Consultations are indispensable in preparing annual budgets, to ascertain and to take account of the priorities of the most influential and responsible members, and to learn what modifications in previous allocations they advocate, what changes they would oppose, their judgments about the need for additional income and the prospects for obtaining it, and their readiness to help.

Individual consultations in advance of board and committee meetings strongly influence what the meetings will decide. Such consultations enable chairpersons and staff members to learn what views will be expressed, what positions will be taken, which of these will differ, and who will air opposing views.

Consultations enable a chairperson and staff member to plan and conduct discussion to obtain the most constructive consideration of issues, and to identify the potential for resolving them. It enables the chairperson and staff member to bring together the leading opposing advocates between meetings, to try to resolve differences, and to work out agreements and compromises that can then be recommended jointly at future meetings to make possible consensus that otherwise could not be achieved.

Officers and staff members diligently consult with the most influential volunteer leaders between meetings to keep them informed of developments, and to obtain their reactions and advice. As volunteers generally welcome being consulted, this underscores their importance to the organizations and deepens their commitment.

Individual consultations are often invaluable in implementing the board's decisions. The knowledge, experience, and relationships of particular volunteers can enable organizations to obtain resources and the cooperation of government, media, business corporations, and others that the staff alone could not secure.

Because individual consultations are critical to the success of an organization, they are carefully and thoroughly planned. Volunteers and staff members who initiate consultations prepare an agenda of what they want to discuss and achieve. The consultations are not casual ad hoc improvisations.

The volunteers and staff members who initiate the consultations know the information they want to convey, the questions they want considered, the positions they want to present, the options they want to test, the requests they want to make (and the supporting reasons), the problems they may encounter, and how they will deal with them.

They understand that the people being consulted will have their own agendas. They try to forecast what those agendas might include and to be prepared to discuss them as knowledgeably as possible.

They conscientiously follow up on the consultations to carry out any promises and commitments they have made. They provide the information that was requested, contact the people they agreed to approach, and take other actions that were projected. They promptly inform the persons consulted about what has been done as a result of the consultations.

The leading organizations, in sum, could not function most effectively without individual consultations. Through them, organizations gain knowledge and understanding; obtain the judgments and guidance of their most resourceful, influential, and respected leaders; deepen their understanding of those leaders; correct misconceptions; analyze differences and resolve many of them; secure critical support for policies and programs they want to advance; and obtain commitments to accept important responsibilities.

Individual consultations require skilled handling to arrange, conduct, implement, and capitalize upon. They require substantial personal investment. The CVO, CPO, volunteer leaders, and staff members budget the time for them, and conscientiously adhere to that schedule.

The CVO and CPO especially instill in other volunteers and staff members an understanding of the necessity and value of individual consultations. They train and supervise those people to carry out such consultations.

Organization officials know, too, that beyond the consultations they schedule and conduct, many individual consultations occur informally among volunteers, among volunteers and staff members, and among professionals, on their own initiative. The officials try to assure that the volunteers and staff are continually as fully informed as possible regarding the organization, so that what is discussed informally is rooted in accurate knowledge and understanding.

The leaders encourage the volunteers and staff members to bring back to the CVO, CPO, officers, and staff the questions, concerns, attitudes, judgments, and misconceptions that have been voiced in the informal discussions, that deserve attention, and that may require action by the organization.

Individual consultations permeate the decision making and actions of advanced, achieving organizations. They are the first priority of newly elected CVOs and CPOs when they begin their responsibilities. The thoroughness with which these organizations initiate, employ, and deepen the consultations are a hallmark of outstanding organizations, as are the gains they derive from them.

18

———•◦•——●——•◦•———

COLLABORATION

Leading nonprofit organizations are team players, not "loners." They consult with each other, cooperate, collaborate, coordinate, and take joint actions. They realize that they are partners with other nonprofits in advancing the public welfare.

They understand that other organizations share their concerns, goals, and purposes. They are aware that other organizations can support what they do, and they enlarge their achievements by collaborating with them and reinforcing their services. On the negative side, they understand that other organizations can obstruct what they do by advocating contrary policies and taking opposing actions, and that they can make their work wasteful by duplicating what they perform.

The leading organizations know that often what they undertake is interdependent with the services of others, that each can alleviate or overcome only part of a problem; that they depend on others to make possible what they do; that there are intertwined aspects of needs that no single organization can resolve unless others share in overcoming the related parts.

> EXAMPLE:
> Many organizations serve the elderly. Some concentrate on economic independence by employing the elderly or helping them to find employment, or by providing vocational training to qualify them for employment. Others are concerned with health issues, providing medical care, treating chronic illness in nursing homes, or transferring the elderly to hospitals temporarily for acute illnesses and then returning them to nursing homes. Other organizations counsel the elderly and their families, provide housing, feed the older population with delivered meals, and offer personal companionship and recreation.

Depending on his or her needs, a single person may be served by several organizations at the same time. As several agencies impact on the same person, what each does affects what the others do. The advanced organizations plan together, coordinate their assistance, and evaluate jointly how effectively they serve.

Throughout the nonprofit sector, volunteer leaders and staff members are in ongoing consultations with those of other organizations. They learn from each other, acquire understanding, share analyses and judgments on major concerns, are enlarged and advanced by each others' expertise and experience. Collaborating organizations have a combined greater range and depth of knowledge and expertise than any single organization alone possesses. Wise organizations regularly draw from and willingly give to each other, in their continuing consultations and collaboration.

Organizations that have closely related and interdependent services share in planning and cooperate in carrying out their services. They jointly project the services that promise the greatest achievement, reinforcing each other as they pursue mutual goals.

They may sponsor united actions when their combined services can accomplish what one could not achieve alone. They link their funds, volunteers, and staffs to overcome their limitations. They understand what Daniel Webster stated many years ago: "Men can do jointly what they cannot do singly; and the union of minds and hands, the concentration of power becomes almost omnipotent."

The foremost organizations readily become members of national umbrella associations in their respective fields—in child care, health, arts, civil rights, and other areas. They gain much from them. They learn of the successes of other organizations, which they can replicate and adapt to accelerate their own progress and achievements; they discover the failures others have encountered, which they take care not to repeat.

They draw from and through their umbrella organizations the highest expertise in their fields to guide and advance their services, build stronger volunteer leadership, recruit and develop quality staffs, upgrade their management, increase their financing, and refine their planning, budgeting, and communication.

Umbrella organizations enable their members to share common concerns; they help build greater local grassroots and national understanding and support for their principles, goals, and services. Individual organizations utilize their umbrella groups to act together as their instruments; utilizing their combined power, they can press for favorable government policies, financing, and services.

In addition to the involvement in their respective umbrella association, leading organizations join in coalitions of organizations that embrace other fields, especially to advocate for what they mutually seek. Such coalitions act together to obtain legislation they favor or prevent legislation they oppose, and to influence government regulations and judicial decisions.

Coalitions inform the public of their current concerns and build support for the positions they advocate. They can be effective in obtaining the editorial influence of the media.

Some coalitions are continuing endeavors that conduct consultations and analyses; formulate shared policies, priorities, and strategies; and take joint actions. Others are ad hoc initiatives, convened to address a particular concern or for concerted action on a specific issue; ad hoc coalitions disband when an action has been completed.

Effective organizations have learned that individual organizations acting independently and competitively can cancel each other out, that they nullify what each seeks if they take opposing positions on issues as they try to obtain the support of the media or actions by government; they understand at minimum the need to consult with each other to share analyses and judgments, to attempt to resolve differences, and to reach agreement if possible on united positions.

In all collaborations, a basic motivation is enlightened self-interest. An advanced organization is impelled by the realization that cooperation will enable it to achieve more of its purposes, that it will be a stronger and more successful organization if it collaborates than it would if it remained isolated.

The collaborative process in itself provides inherent gains. The experience of meeting and working with others enlarges the knowledge of the participants, and provides a testing ground for their concerns, judgments, and new ideas. It establishes invaluable professional relationships that become continuing resources. It wins new friends and supporters. It brings an organization greater recognition, enhanced prestige, and greater respect because of what other groups learn about it.

Teamwork is a mutual sharing process. Each organization has input in shaping what is decided and what is done. Each avoids arbitrary domination by other organizations, and requires genuine openness and full consideration of all views. Each organization retains its full autonomy and carries out only what it agrees to do. Each can withdraw from a joint body whenever it may decide to do so; the fact that an organization rarely does so is because in such collaborations autonomy is generally respected and because each group generally benefits greatly.

Organizations collaborate in coalitions on issues and concerns on which they agree. On other matters not within the compass of the coalition, they can oppose each other vigorously. Thus, Catholic Charities and Planned Parenthood can work together on what both seek as members of Independent Sector, while differing vigorously on abortion, which is not part of the Independent Sector agenda.

Advanced organizations are actively involved in their umbrella groups, coordinating bodies, and coalitions. They are not merely passive names on letterheads. They take the lead in creating coalitions where they are needed, and in urging other organizations to join. They bring their concerns and views to the joint bodies. Their representatives diligently attend the meetings, actively take part in the discussions, present and evaluate options, help carry out the decisions, join in evaluating what is done, and share in encouraging and guiding further collaboration.

Successful organizations try to make sure that their collaborative investment of funds, time, and energies is productive. They prevent interminable, fruitless, and wasteful discussions and meetings. They require that each joint meeting must advance the issue at hand, and must be substantive and productive.

They understand that collaboration will continue only if there are tangible results, and that the collaboration will collapse if there is only a series of frustrations and failures. They set ambitious but realistic targets, and have a high rate of success in achieving them.

19

GOVERNMENT
RELATIONS

Nonprofit organizations are vitally impacted by government policies and actions on human needs. They are
affected by tax deductions for the contributions that basically support them; by government grants that finance some
of their services; by tax exemptions, regulations, judicial
decisions, and laws; and by administrative rulings that control their lobbying. They are affected by the responsibilities
government takes for human needs and by what it neglects.

Nonprofit organizations are not passive subjects of the
decisions government makes. The leading organizations vigorously advocate what they believe government should do
and oppose government actions that could be destructive.

Tax deductions for the contributions that finance non-profits are continuously threatened. Legislation is intro-duced in every session of the U.S. Congress to reduce these deductions, which potentially can cause great losses to the organizations. Changes in tax rates in recent years have cost nonprofits billions of dollars, as a number of large donors have reduced the amounts of their gifts. Many millions more were lost when Congress eliminated charitable deductions by the vast majority of taxpayers who do not itemize their annual income tax returns. Even more was lost when Con-gress temporarily restricted deductions of gifts in kind to the original costs of the gifts of securities and art, as opposed to their current market value. Nonprofit organizations have succeeded in getting the deductibility of the market value restored, and they are working to have the deductions by nonitemizers reinstated.

Nonprofits continue to find it necessary to overcome the false premise underlying the attempts to cut back the de-ductions: the myth that the government loses income equivalent to the amount of the tax deductions and that the deductions are therefore actually government expenditures. That premise is based on the fiction that if donors did not make their deductions, the government would collect the equivalent amount of funds. It neglects the demonstrated reality that donors have many other ways to utilize those funds without paying taxes on them and that the govern-ment therefore would not obtain all of them.

Nonprofit organizations understand that many massive social problems are far beyond their financial capacity to overcome. Only the government has the financial ability to address them. Nonprofit organizations historically have sen-sitized legislators to such needs, have helped the lawmakers understand them, have formulated legislation to overcome them, pressed the legislators to enact it, and have monitored the implementation of services to assure that services are effective.

They have sounded alarms when services were inadequate and when threatened changes would reduce or undermine them, and have led the opposition to such retrogression.

Government has often chosen nonprofit organizations to perform services rather than have government render them because of the expertise, economies, and efficiency that the nonprofit organizations can provide.

Some 30 percent of the income of nonprofit organizations for serving social needs comes from government. The proportion is especially great for hospitals, universities, childcare organizations, and agencies serving the elderly. It is critical support.

These organizations have to work with legislators to match the support with the needs, to take account of inflationary increased costs, and to prevent ruinous cuts. They research legislative changes to learn what funds are available to them. They have developed skills in applying for and obtaining such support.

The organizations have had to make unending efforts to maintain their nonprofit postal rates, in the face of legislative proposals to increase them.

They have had to resist the pressures of the small business lobby to have government tax museums, homes for the aged, hospitals, and other institutions on sales by their gift shops, whose income has become essential in offsetting recent cutbacks in government grants and losses from tax deduction changes.

On another front, the tax exemptions of nonprofit organizations are constantly threatened by local governments, who sometimes float proposals to have the organizations pay property taxes and other municipal costs.

The efforts of various states to place ceilings on fund-raising costs have been a recurring problem, especially for new organizations, whose initial costs to get off the ground are higher than those of established organizations. Nonprofits have taken the issue to the Supreme Court and have won a ruling that prevents such ceilings. But efforts to set such ceilings continue.

Nonprofit organizations have taken and continue to take other issues to the courts, as plaintiffs and in submitting friend-of-the-court briefs.

Government regulations impact nonprofit organizations in a host of ways. They set requirements for their governance; for their pensions and tax-deferred salaries; for their financial reporting; for possible conflicts of interest by their officers, board members, and staffs. The organizations guide the government on regulations that should be enacted, as well as on harmful ones that should be modified and prevented.

The ability of nonprofits to influence government is constantly subject to proposed laws and regulations to limit their lobbying. The proposals challenge one of the fundamental purposes and responsibilities of the nonprofit sector, namely to serve as a conscience for government, in the alleviation and overcoming of human problems, and in building and maintaining a compassionate, caring, and just society. They have led the government to a number of historic advances, including our basic social-welfare programs, Social Security, Medicare, civil rights, and protection of the environment.

Each year, nonprofit organizations have had to deal with legislation that would penalize the entire sector because of the abuses of a few organizations that have spent the bulk of their income for fund raising and very little for service or that have used funds for purposes other than those for which they were solicited. The nonprofit sector has vigorously supported legislation and regulations to assure the highest ethics and integrity in their finances and services, but have opposed penalties and restrictions that would penalize the innocent.

In all of these efforts, nonprofit organizations act for what is best for the entire sector, and not alone for themselves or their own field. They know that any advantage in government provisions they may have over other organizations is not only unjust but will soon disappear.

> EXAMPLE:
> When legislation was proposed to cut back on
> tax deductions for most nonprofit organizations
> while retaining them for hospitals and
> universities, the hospitals and universities
> vigorously opposed it, despite their own
> exemption. The legislation was defeated.

Nonprofit organizations manifestly have been proactive, not merely reactive, in their relations with government. They have initiated legislation, regulations, and court actions, have pressed for them, and have obtained them.

Because of their stake in government policies, responsibilities, financing, and controls, the leading organizations have made government relations one of their primary programs. Such issues figure prominently on their board-meeting agendas, in order to keep the board informed and to allow for analysis of the concerns, the formulation of positions, and the taking of action on them.

They assure continuing top-level attention to government relations by having qualified committees keep fully alert to the concerns and opportunities they should address, prepare the analyses they need, and give oversight to the actions they authorize. They assign professional responsibility to competent staff members who understand legislative process and become skilled in utilizing it.

They know how important the local impact of proposed national legislation is to their own congressmen, and they have made sure that their legislators are fully informed of its grassroots effects. Crucial congressional decisions have been determined when the congressmen visit their home districts and learn what the legislation would do to their own universities, hospitals, services for the elderly, and other institutions.

The organizations send delegations to Washington and to their state capitols to meet with legislators. They testify before legislative committees. They meet with their representatives when their legislators are in their communities. They invite them to their meetings to gain a first-hand knowledge of what they do. They maintain year-round contacts, building and strengthening their relationships. They do not limit their contacts to crises or special appeals.

They have volunteer leaders and other influential citizens who know their legislators contact them personally. Such personal contacts are often more effective than any other actions the organizations can take.

The leaders and staffs of the organizations meet with the editors of their newspapers, and with the news anchorpersons of their radio and television stations, to build their understanding of issues and to gain their support for what the organizations advocate. They submit op-ed pieces and letters to newspapers and magazines.

In addition to what organizations do individually, they work through their local and national umbrella organizations to act collectively for what they seek. They form and join coalitions to collaborate with other organizations locally, state-wide, and nationally for their mutual goals.

In sum, their government relations activities enable organizations to carry out their missions, perform the humanitarian services to which they are dedicated, and help build the principled, compassionate, just society to which all are dedicated.

20

---·—•—·---

RELATED AND INTERDEPENDENT

The practices we have analyzed are related and interdependent. Each can be carried out productively because the others make them possible. Each depends on the others. Each reinforces the others.

Mission

Their defined missions control and focus everything non-profit organizations do. The mission concentrates their responsibilities, functions, and services. It determines what they include and what they exclude. It establishes the qualifications of who will comprise their constituencies, their volunteer governing board, their professional staffs.

Human Resources

An organization's human resources—its volunteers and staff—are pivotal in every aspect of what it is and does. Advanced nonprofits are leaders because of the excellence, deep commitment, and active involvement of their volunteers and the expertise of their professionals. These two groups determine their policies, wisely and responsibly administer them, resolve the major issues that confront them, and effectively implement what they vote.

Throughout, there is a close, harmonious partnership of volunteers and professionals. The ablest volunteers insist on having outstanding professional staffs; the staffs make certain that they have the most capable volunteer leaders.

Because people more than anything else determine the quality and success of an organization, the highest priority of the leading organizations is to obtain and retain the best volunteers and professional staffs they can secure.

Finance

We have noted, too, that just as human resources are the heart of nonprofit organizations, financing is their lifeblood, for funds make possible their services. In turn, their human resources make possible their funds. The eminence and influence of the volunteer leaders and professional staffs— the respect, confidence, and trust they enjoy, and their own standard-setting contributions—are crucial in attracting generous financing.

Their generous gifts bespeak their own deep commitment, and critically influence the level of support from their peers and from foundations, corporations, and government. Their active, thorough, and skilled solicitation of contributions from others transforms potential resources into actual support. Their expert staff support them in planning and obtaining the financing.

Change

Volunteers and staff are constantly alert to emerging new needs and opportunities that may affect their services, finances, management, and administration. Their openness and readiness to review what they do stems not only from their creativity but from the diverse membership of the boards and committees that leading organizations have carefully developed. The differences within the boards and committees compel a continuing assessment of what the organizations are and do. They engender flexibility in responding to changing circumstances and recasting services, and in initiating change and replacing what new needs and knowledge have shown to be outmoded.

Budgeting

Financing is underpinned and shaped by budgeting. Budgeting specifies the needs the organizations address, and the services they will perform to overcome or ameliorate them. The budgets are governed by the organizations' missions and directed to their central purposes and goals. They articulate the priorities the organizations have set as they strive to reach their goals.

Planning

Budgets are based on planning, which assesses the needs organizations seek to meet, the goals they want to achieve, and their priorities. Planning takes account of what progress has been made to date in addressing needs and goals, the prospects for further achievement, and the ability of an organization's staff, volunteers, and finances to have an impact on those prospects.

Nonprofits plan thoroughly before they approve expenditures for new and untried services, to maximize the likelihood of success and minimize the possibility of failure.

Budgeting and planning are so interdependent that a number of organizations have combined their planning and budget committees. The committees include major contributors and foremost solicitors, so that their projections carry with them the understanding, agreement, and commitment of those primarily responsible for providing the required funds.

Involvement

The intensive involvement of volunteers in defining missions, in obtaining and retaining the ablest volunteers and staff, in financing, in making essential changes, and in budgeting and planning is part of their pervasive involvement in all elements of an organization's operation—the governance, determination of policies, resolution of major issues, oversight of management and services, and carrying out of decisions. Volunteers are not "rubber stamps" for the views of the CVO or CPO. Volunteers genuinely deliberate and develop the organization's decisions and actions.

Facts and Analyses

Financing, planning, budgeting, decision making, and the shaping of all operations are based on the fullest foundation of facts the organizations can obtain. They want to be sure that all participants have a common base of knowledge, to the extent possible, on which to form their judgments. Research to provide facts is indispensable. It need not be an organization's own research; it can be what has been learned by others.

Understanding Nonprofits

A solid base of facts is required for deliberations, but decisions are not based on facts alone. Decisions are shaped by personal values and goals. In working to resolve differences and arrive at consensus, advanced organizations have found it imperative for volunteers and staff to understand the uniqueness of nonprofits and how they differ from business and government. That understanding is essential for all responsibilities. The lack of it has been the cause of many difficulties in less-successful organizations.

Implementation

Implementation of decisions is rooted in how they were arrived at. Involvement of the decision makers is the key, in this as in so many other responsibilities. If it is their decision, if they feel that they "own" it, if the decision reflects their commitment, they actively work to have it financed and carried out.

Monitoring

They then also insist on having the implementation monitored, to make sure that it carries out what they authorized and projected. Having taken responsibility for the decisions and for financing what was authorized, they want to detect any shortcomings as quickly as possible, to find their causes and to make corrections and adjustments promptly, so that their funds are not wasted and their efforts succeed.

Evaluations

Beyond ongoing monitoring, leading nonprofits increasingly conduct comprehensive evaluations of their services, to determine what impact they have made on the needs and purposes they address. They conduct internal evaluations by their volunteers and staffs, and in some cases bring in expert, outside analysts to appraise what has been done. In addition to evaluations of particular services and fields of operations, a number of organizations make periodic reviews of their entire operations.

They are not deterred by the difficulty that some aspects of their work cannot be measured quantitatively, and that a complexity of many intangible elements must be taken into account. Rather they continuously refine the tools of evaluation to overcome the obstacles, and produce an increasing body of criteria on which to base assessments. They are enabling the organizations to refine and to project their services and operations for the years ahead, guiding changes and priorities in their services and how they administer them.

Communication

Ongoing communication—among volunteers; between volunteers and staff members; among staff; and with contributors, constituents, the media, and the public—is a must for leading nonprofits. It is a requirement for their internal operations and their external relations.

Each volunteer and staff member is part of a common, shared effort. Communication keeps each informed of what the others are doing and how that will impact on their own work. Communication informs them of developments that affect each of them; informs constituents about what an organization's board and staff are doing on their behalf; reports to contributors on how their funds are being applied to the purposes for which they were donated and what is being accomplished through their support.

Communication builds an understanding in the media and the public of an organization's services and how those services affect the community's human needs and improve the quality of life.

Communication informs government officials about the work of nonprofits and how that work is related to government responsibilities, services, and financing of human needs. Communication alerts government officials to unmet needs and advises them on actions required to address those needs.

Another important aspect of communication are the questions, concerns, and advice of an organization's constituents and contributors bring to its officers, board members, and staff; these observations can help shape an organization's direction, priorities, and services.

Consultations with Individuals

Consultations with individuals are vital in virtually all elements of an advanced organization's procedures, deliberations, and actions. Yet they are often neglected by struggling and less-successful nonprofits. Internal consultations—between the CVO and CPO, among the officers, board members, with major contributors, and with leaders of opposing positions on major policies and issues—are essential. External consultations—with officials of other organizations and government, with key media people, and with influential citizens—are equally important.

Consultations are necessary to recruit outstanding volunteers and staff members, undertake changes and innovations in services, obtain financial support, make board and committee meetings productive, achieve consensus on difficult issues, secure the cooperation of other organizations in forming coalitions on shared purposes, gain government approval for desired legislation and regulations, and defeat destructive proposals.

Teamwork

Teamwork is a hallmark of leading organizations. In effective organizations, teamwork exists among the volunteers, in the staffs, and between volunteers and staff. Each person readily informs others of what he or she is doing, consults on shared concerns, and meets in groups to learn from each other, pool judgments, and work out next steps. Each person pitches in to help the others handle pressures and emergencies; doors are open, individual turf is not marked out or tenaciously protected; all collaborate, reinforcing one another and adding to the cumulative achievement.

The same attitude and principles motivate relations with other organizations. There is willing cooperation to assist and learn from one another, and to collaborate on joint actions for shared purposes. Such cooperation is rooted in the understanding that everyone is working to overcome critical human problems, that each individual can achieve only a part of that goal, that what each person does affects what the others can accomplish, and that all of them are trying to improve life for the community and society.

Relations with government, too, are regarded as a partnership and not a competition. The nonprofits are aware that neither they alone nor government alone can provide all the vital human services, and that government and non-profit organizations must complement each other's efforts, not duplicate them. They also understand that nonprofit organizations historically have provided the leadership to pioneer advances and stimulate the government to accept and adjust responsibilities to overcome previous neglect and to advance the goals to be accomplished.

Ethics

In everything they do, the nonprofit organizations must be committed to the highest ethical standards. They require honesty and integrity in every element of their operation and deplore the occasional deviations of a few organizations that undermine confidence and trust in the entire sector.

The organizations carry out the services for which they obtained their funds and endeavor to apportion costs of services and administration to assure the utmost effectiveness. No volunteers profit financially from their involvement in the organizations. Nonprofits have set up explicit safeguards against conflicts of interest in any volunteer or staff member. Their finances are audited by certified public accountants. They report openly and regularly on their finances and services.

The organizations seek to serve as models of integrity, to meet the highest requirements of legality, and even more, to satisfy the highest principles of morality. They want and need to earn and maintain the confidence and trust of their constituents and the public, so that their conduct matches the nobility of their goals.

INDEX

capital funds, 46–47
from corporations, 44, 45
cost ceilings, 162–63
effects of tax laws, 47–48,
160, 163
endowment funds, 43–44
from foundations, 44–45
goals, 40
government grants, 45–46
individual consultations,
148
planned giving, 43–44
reports to donors, 139–40,
143
soliciting prospects, 41–42
staff, 39
from volunteers, 41,
168–69

Gardner, John, 117–18
governing bodies
committee reports to,
85–86, 117, 122–25,
139
communicating with
constituencies, 69–70
communicating with
members, 143
crisis management, 125–26
decisions, 125
diverse membership, 65,
69, 99–105, 169
fund raising and, 39–41
government relations
issues, 163–64, 175
meetings, 149
members, 14–15, 95–97
nominating committees,
15, 68
obstacles to resolving
issues, 105–17
orientation programs, 69
personal relationships in,
96–97, 110
personnel committees,
24–25

relationship with chief
professional officers
(CPOs), 32
resolving issues, 89–92
selection of chief
professional officers,
23–24
term limits, 16
training for, 16
government
contracts with, 161
grants, 45–46
lobbying, 162
local and state, 161, 164
regulations, 162
relations with, 159–65, 173,
175
social programs, 160–61
tax laws, 160, 161, 163
Gray, Sandra, 138

human resources. See
professional staff;
volunteers

implementation of decisions
financing, 131
flexibility in, 128–29
individual consultations in,
150
involvement of decision
makers, 171
monitoring, 133–35, 172
oversight committees,
130–31, 134, 138, 139
planning, 128
quality of, 127–28
staff responsible for,
129–30, 131–32
income
fees for services, 46
sources, 38
See also fund raising
individual consultations,
147–51
agendas, 150

professional staff
  analysis of options by,
    119–20
  collegiality, 26
  communications experts,
    142
  communication with, 145
  compensation, 24
  fund-raising experts, 39
  government relations, 164
  management of, 24, 25,
    26, 35, 151
  morale, 26
  personnel codes, 24–25
  relations with volunteers,
    27–31, 35–36, 168,
    174–75
  research projects, 59–60,
    92
  responsible for
    implementations,
    129–30, 131–32
  selecting, 129–30
  training, 78
  vested interests, 108
  working with committees,
    77–80, 81–83, 86, 87,
    88, 101, 148
  See also chief professional
    officers (CPOs)
programs
  collaborating with other
    nonprofits, 155
  evaluating, 135–38, 172
  fees, 46
  government, 160–61
  monitoring, 133–35, 172
  pressures for new, 8
  protecting existing, 107–8
  See also implementation
    of decisions
progress reports, 122–24
public foundations, 44

reports
  annual, 143

of committees to board,
    85–86, 117, 122–25, 139
  confidential, 123–24
  to donors, 42, 139–40, 143
  financial, 143, 176
  progress, 122–24
  See also communication
research
  outside experts, 58, 59, 92
  purpose, 58, 60, 171
  qualitative, 58–59
  volunteer and staff
    involvement, 59–60, 92

search committees, 23–24
services. See programs
speakers, providing, 145
staff. See professional staff;
    support staff
supporting foundations, 44
support staff, 26

taxes
  deductions for
    contributions, 160, 163
  effects on contributions,
    47–48
  exemptions from local, 161
  on income of nonprofits,
    161
teamwork, 174–75
technology
  communications, 142–43
  computers, 58

umbrella organizations,
    155–56, 157–58, 164
U.S. Congress
  communicating with
    representatives, 164
  tax law changes, 160
U.S. Supreme Court, 162

vested interests, 108